HELLO!

I'm Stuart, AKA Ashens. I make videos for YouTube, write comedy scripts and sometimes act in things.
When I realised that I missed writing articles and stories, I joined forces with Unbound to rectify that by writing books.
I live in Norwich, in a house filled with all sorts of useless items that I tell myself I need for my work. I'm obsessed with old video games and things that aren't quite good enough for their intended purpose.
My favourite soup is crab meat and sweetcorn.

@ashens
youtube.com/ashens

TERRIBLE OLD GAMES
YOU'VE PROBABLY
NEVER HEARD OF

TERRIBLE OLD GAMES YOU'VE PROBABLY NEVER HEARD OF

STUART ASHEN

unbound

FIRST PUBLISHED IN 2015

This paperback edition first published in 2020

Unbound
6th Floor, Mutual House, 70 Conduit Street, London
W1S 2GF

www.unbound.com

Text Design by Friederike Huber
Art direction by Friederike Huber

A CIP record for this book is available from the
British Library

ISBN 978-1-78352-938-4 (trade pbk)
ISBN 978-1-78352-256-9 (trade hbk)
ISBN 978-1-78352-257-6 (ebook)
ISBN 978-1-78352-266-8 (limited edition)

Printed in Spain by Novoprint

9 8 7 6 5 4 3 2 1

This book is dedicated to anyone who ever bought a terrible game, wiped the tape with a magnet, then took it back to the shop.

SUPERFRIENDS LIST

Listed here are the Superfriends –
people who pledged a substantial
amount of money to help ensure that
this book became a reality. May their
game cassettes never demagnetise.

Leo Baggerreft
Michael Barrett
Alan Boyd
Michael Brown
Dua9in Cameron
Gregor Cameron
Christopher Cobb
Chloe Cresswell
Thomas Edge
Matthew Faulkner
Brent Friedrich
Sam Glennie
Alex "Peggy" Grant
Richard "dragonridley" Hatton
Ian Hopkins
Daniel Fink Jensen
Trent Johnson
Joshua Kahn
Joseph Kawa
Lucas Kmiecik
Kymo Misenica Kobayashi
Ephraim Leadon
Marko Mannonen
Matthew Mitchell
Tanja "Tikal" Pattberg
Jeroen Richters
Dominic Rossetto-White
Aidan Rothnie
Nathan Schlosser
Aaron Scott
Mike Sleeman
Sam Thompson
Mark Tolladay
Tommy Törnqvist :)
Justin Trueland
Adam Unwin
Sean Zoltek

CONTENTS

INTRODUCTION
BY STUART ASHEN

HELLO! And welcome to *Terrible Old Games You've Probably Never Heard Of*, a compendium of some of the most obscure and appalling titles spewed out by the video games industry.

This isn't a guide to the very worst – it's a showcase for games that I personally found intriguing as well as mind-bleedingly awful. I've included a variety of game types and release formats, and largely ignored the prices to find objectively awful games. And most importantly, you won't find the usual suspects like *E.T.* for the Atari 2600 and *Superman* for the Nintendo 64 as they're already covered extensively on many different websites and YouTube videos.

For inclusion in this book, a game must have been:
· Released some time between 1980–1995 inclusive
· Sold commercially
· Released for a home computer format, not a games console*
· So utterly terrible that it would be almost impossible for a reasonable person to enjoy playing the game.

A lot of games we played thirty years ago seem crap now, but *Terrible Old Games You've Probably Never Heard Of* is about the ones that were crap then.

I've also asked some knowledgeable and interesting people what the most disappointing game they ever bought was. Those won't necessarily be terrible games, but they will have made people angry which is as equally entertaining. I even allowed mention of a Nintendo game as it provides a great point about what gaming was like before the Internet.

Giant heaps full of thanks go to the people who pledged to get this book published via Unbound. Now the games mentioned inside will finally receive the recognition and derision they deserve – because they're terrible, they're old, and you probably haven't heard of them.

Stuart Ashen
Norwich, 2015

For the purposes of this book I've counted the Commodore Amiga CD32 as a computer, because it's essentially an Amiga 1200 with the keyboard chopped off and a CD drive stuck on. So there.

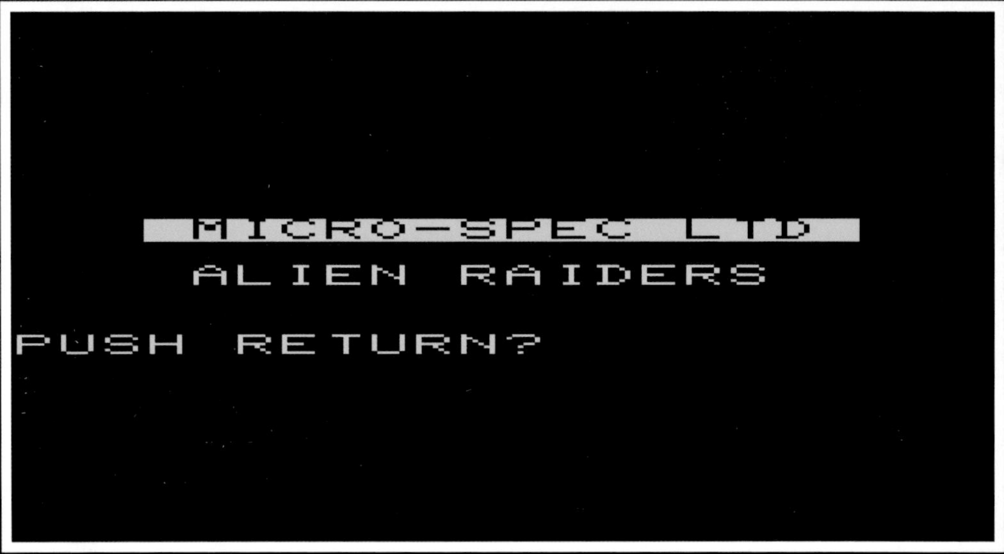

ALIEN RAIDERS

FORMAT: COMMODORE VIC-20
YEAR OF RELEASE: APPROX. 1983
DEVELOPER: HARTEVELD SOFTWARE
PUBLISHER: MICRO-SPEC LTD
ORIGINAL PRICE: UNKNOWN

The fun never starts in Alien Raiders! Or Alien Invaders, for that matter.

THERE'S CONFUSION with this game before it even starts. The title screen calls the game *Alien Raiders*, but the next screen calls it *Alien Invaders* – a name also shown at the top of the screen during the game! For the purposes of this book, I'm going with *Alien Raiders* as that's what was written on the cartridge, but either name is valid I suppose. If only video games had birth certificates.

The first thing *Alien Raiders* does is

assault you with four seconds of random beeping, which is never a nice thing to experience. It then tells you the controls for left, right and fire, and away you go into possibly the most worthless single-screen shoot 'em up ever made.

You control a classic *Space Invaders* style ship that sits on a black line. Four green alien ships jerk down the screen extremely slowly. Occasionally two aliens will start in the same place, which

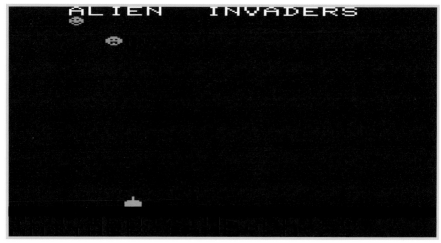

The inevitable outcome of playing Alien Raiders. The correct answer is "NO".

leads to one of them disappearing and there only being three on screen for the rest of the game. They move straight down, one at a time from left to right, then sit still for a second before the movement wave starts again. Your ship moves much faster and can shoot straight up, with a single bullet on screen at any time. When you shoot an enemy ship it turns into a black waffle that blocks your shots until the next time the aliens move, although sometimes they remain on screen until an alien moves over them. When an alien is shot, it's replaced with another from the top of the screen.

Soundwise, *Alien Raiders* makes only two noises after the initial random beeping. There's a warble when you shoot and a sound like spit hitting a tom-tom drum when an alien is hit.

The game is written in BASIC, and

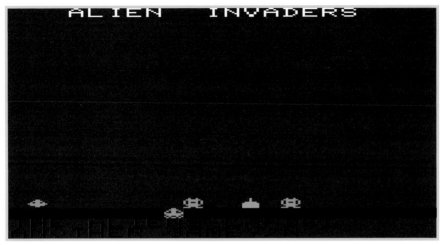

You won't see this message unless you really want to or if you're the victim of an annoying bug.

both the aliens and your ship only move along the 8x8 character blocks of the VIC's standard screen mode. The result is there are only 20 horizontal positions the aliens can be in, and your ship is restricted to the same columns they travel down. A combination of this restriction, the aliens' inability to move sideways, and the speed of your ship means *Alien Raiders* is painfully easy. It's a very simple task to line yourself up under the extraterrestrial idiots, and you have absolutely ages to do it. If one of the invading raiders reaches the bottom of the screen, it's instantly game over, but that's not going to happen unless you deliberately allow it.

This leads us into the game's strangest design choice. When you shoot an alien, you receive 10 points. When you accumulate 100 points, you

All of the alien types. I call them Harold, Susan, Engelbert, Boffo and Revenge of Boffo.

win and the game immediately ends. So all you have to do is shoot ten aliens, which takes approximately 36 seconds. It's so easy that I managed to easily complete three versions of the game at once by simultaneously running multiple VIC-20 emulators.

The only chance of losing without it being on purpose is if you encounter a bug that makes the aliens invisible when you shoot them – they sometimes become impossible to shoot and will just progress down the screen unless you can get the score to 100 first. Otherwise, you effectively have to choose to lose. Also, when the game ends, it asks if you want to play again with a Y/N prompt – but entering Y ends the program; you have to enter the whole word YES. Not that anyone

would likely want to play the game more than once, but it's annoying anyway.

Alien Raiders is an absolute swindle. It's 36 seconds of utterly tedious gameplay for what was almost certainly a premium price, as it was released on an expensive cartridge rather than a cassette tape.

The game is also a bit of an enigma. It consists of only 88 lines of BASIC code. Was it designed as a game for toddlers? Was it a magazine type-in that somehow got released commercially? And who was the publisher Micro-Spec? There's no record of them releasing anything other than this game.

A look at the source code reveals an extra final line numbered 65000 that

```
      ALIEN   INVADERS
  INSTRUCTIONS:
    <              =  LEFT
    >              =  RIGHT
  LEFT SHIFT  =  FIRES

  PRESS  RETURN
```

says "Harteveld Software" surrounded with asterisks. Harteveld were a Dutch developer who released the puzzle games *Kolom Raden* (Guess the Column) and *Memory* – both simple BASIC games and both of which have the same line 65000 in them. It therefore seems likely they made a game called *Alien Invaders* that they never released themselves, but that for some reason Micro-Spec published as *Alien Raiders*. What is the story behind the whole affair? We may never know… or care.

REVIEW SCORES
None known.

OTHER VERSIONS
None. Just play any version of Space Invaders on any machine and you'll almost certainly have more fun.

ALIEN SIDESTEP

FORMAT: COMMODORE 64
YEAR OF RELEASE: 1983
DEVELOPER: UNKNOWN. VIC-20 VERSION

This is Strategy Alpha. During Level 2. You will probably be asleep by this point.

SPACE INVADERS WAS A worldwide phenomenon, but five years after release it was getting a little stale. The time had come to put a new spin on a classic. And who better to do that than Mr Computer Products? The answer, tragically, is *anybody.*

It's been said that the key to a good game is choice. Some games offer multiple ways to beat a challenge, but even the simplest examples need you to make the right choice at the right time to win. Do you move left or right? Do you fire one last time or retreat to the side? Or do you play *Alien Sidestep*, which effectively eliminates player choice and therefore any potential fun?

This is Strategy Omega. And also the least impressive firework display in history.

Rows of aliens appear on the screen from the top left. They move horizontally to the right, at which point they reappear at the left further down. If they reach the bottom of the screen, then it is officially a bad thing, because the game ends if it happens three times. Nothing revolutionary so far.

BUT! The aliens have mastered the dark art of the sidestep, a bit like the drivers in the fourth *The Fast and the Furious* movie. This means that when they are about to be hit by a bullet, they stop moving so it passes harmlessly to their right, which presents a *massive* problem. The bullets fired from your

These are all the enemy types. They are worth 10, 20 and 30 points respectively, and they are all suspiciously familiar.

crude blue rocket crawl painfully slowly up the screen and you can only have 16 on the screen at once. This means the usual tactic of aiming at where the aliens will be is useless, as they just stop moving before they're hit.

In fact, to actually progress in *Alien Sidestep*, there are only two effective battle plans. I shall refer to them as Strategy Alpha and Strategy Omega, and both rely on shooting a bullet directly to the left of the previous bullet.

STRATEGY ALPHA:

1. Move from the left of the screen to the right, hammering the fire button so there isn't a gap in your bullets for the aliens to slip through.
2. Move your ship back to the left as your bullets crawl up the screen.
3. Repeat steps 1 and 2 forever.

STRATEGY OMEGA:

1. Move your ship slightly to the left, then slightly to the right, firing constantly.
2. Repeat step 1 forever.

And that's it! Any divergence from either strategy will result in not shooting anything, and ultimately game over. And Strategy Alpha is far more effective than Strategy Omega, so you can't even mix it up by swapping between them without risking failure. There is no room for deviation, improvisation or fun.

The depressingly repetitive gameplay is further reinforced by a total lack of variety in the game's levels. Shoot enough of the *Space Invader* rip-off aliens on level 1 and you will get to shoot identically-acting aliens that look slightly different on levels

ALIEN SIDESTEP

Made in USA

Mr.Computer Products
O.E.M. inc.

This is the actual game label. Notice the inexplicable wavy quiff encroaching bottom centre.

2 and 3. And if you complete level 3, then the words "POINTS DOUBLE" appear on screen and the charge fanfare that Scrappy-Doo loved so much plays. Then everything starts all over again. And because it never gets more difficult, it's pretty much impossible to lose if you follow Strategy Alpha. You could actually play *Alien Sidestep* forever – the only real obstacle is maintaining interest through the mind-crushing tedium.

There is only one unpredictable feature in the entire game – sometimes, if you hit an alien (usually on the top row) you get 50 points and the little "you've picked up an item or jumped a barrel!" tune from *Donkey Kong* plays. It seems to happen at random and is not even 0.001% enough to save the game from being a boring, monotonous chore.

Alien Sidestep was released by Mr Computer Products (also known as O.E.M. Inc.), who may well rank as one of the worst game publishers in history. They released about eight games, all in 1983, and they're all rubbish at best. *Alien Sidestep* wasn't even their worst effort – that accolade goes to *Close Encounters of the Worst Kind*, an astonishingly honest title for a game that is simply a shrieking, pulsating mess of sprites that seems specifically designed to induce a headache.

The much nicer VIC-20 version. Still no fun to play, though.

REVIEW SCORES
None known.

OTHER VERSIONS
Commodore VIC-20: All of Mr Computer Products' games were also available on the VIC-20, with the possible exception of their dire *Donkey Kong* rip-off *Mario's Brewery*. In fact, their C64 titles seem to be bad ports of the VIC-20 originals! Despite the C64 being a much more powerful machine, its version of *Alien Sidestep* is slower, jerkier and has annoying sprite flickering. The VIC-20 version has a lower resolution but is otherwise superior in every way.

BATTLE PROBE

FORMAT: ATARI ST
YEAR OF RELEASE: 1988
DEVELOPER: CAPITAL SOFTWARE DESIGNS LTD
PUBLISHER: CRYSYS
ORIGINAL PRICE: 14.99 POUNDS

That's a very unconvincing star field. The skulls are quite good though.

to be a Russian poem automatically translated into English by faulty software. I don't know if it helped sales, but I suspect not.

A simple, vertically-scrolling shoot 'em up, *Battle Probe* has you controlling a spaceship, flying over space stations of some kind as enemy ships attack you. The only slight deviation from the basic template is that your ship has an ever-diminishing fuel supply you need to replenish, although it never came close to running out when I was playing.

Battle Probe is an amazingly orange game. The status area is orange. Your ship is orange. Most enemies are orange. The backgrounds are orange. Your bullets are orange. *Even the stars are orange.* This game is more orange than a clownfish addicted to fake tanning lotion.

And so Human Kind went out of Earth and, like locust, spread and devoured the Galaxy. The Earth was contaminated but out of the contamination there evolved a new life form which regenerated the land, sea and air until once again greedy Human Kind attempted to return.

That's the text from the back of *Battle Probe's* disk case. The usual idea for a case is to write an exciting description of the game to entice browsers to buy it. But publisher Crysys decided to provide what seems

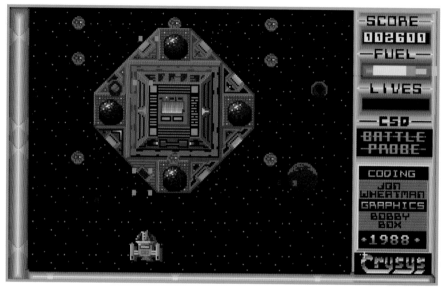

This emplacement exists to shoot eight eyes into space simultaneously. Warfare in the future is weird.

The graphics themselves are generally well defined, but it can be hard to discern what's going on as so many things are the same colour. There are also a lot of eyes featured. Some enemy ships are eyes, gun turrets spew eyes at you, and different coloured eyes in the backgrounds confer extra lives, fuel and bonus points. If I had to create a single image to sum up this game, it would be an orange eye.

When I first loaded *Battle Probe*, I was impressed with how smooth the scrolling and the ship's movements were. My positive impressions ended there, sadly.

As soon as a few enemies appear on screen, the whole game slows to a crawl. Your ship moves so slowly anyway that it's almost impossible to dodge things fired at you. The collision detection – one of the most important parts of a shoot 'em up – is absolutely atrocious, with bullets frequently passing through your ship. Sometimes after losing a life, you restart on a bullet or background obstacle and die again immediately. It's difficult to tell which background objects can be passed over and which

The player's ship narrowly avoids a space satsuma as two eyeball enemies pass over the game's border, possibly in an attempt to escape into the real world.

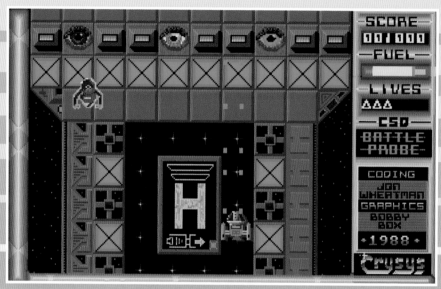

A row of bonus eyeballs. They trigger the spoken phrases "Another ship!", "Bonus!" and "Gas-o-line!"

will kill you. All the enemy ships have identical attack patterns, appearing in threes and waving left and right. The upshot is that *Battle Probe* is no fun to play whatsoever.

Interestingly for the time, the sound consists entirely of sampled audio. The title screen constantly plays a scratchy three second music loop which grates on the nerves after a few plays. The vast majority of the game is silent, punctuated by an explosion effect when an enemy is killed or your ship is destroyed. There are also three different snippets of speech reserved for when you pick up items, although they're almost unintelligible – more due to their odd intonation than

ATARI ST

BATTLE PROBE

The box art isn't particularly noteworthy; I just wanted to use a picture that isn't mostly orange.

forming a new company called New Dimensions. They then made two very weak games before finding their strength in application software – they went on to release the immensely successful *Technosound Turbo* audio sampler for the Amiga, which dance group *The Prodigy* used in their early work.

Publisher Crysys only released *Battle Probe* and three dull sports management games that all used the same game engine. By 1989 they'd disappeared, which was probably for the best.

the low sample quality.

Battle Probe is a depressingly fun-free experience. The whole package feels painfully cheap, especially considering the substantial £15 asking price. There isn't even a game over message – it just cuts abruptly back to the title screen and the three second music loop.

The developers, Capital Software, produced only *Battle Probe* before

REVIEW SCORES
The only magazine to review Battle Probe was ST Action, who awarded it a generous 25%.

OTHER VERSIONS
None. Possibly no other computers could handle so much orange on screen at once.

THE MOST DISAPPOINTING GAME I EVER BOUGHT
BY ALAN BOISTON, RACING GAME JOURNALIST AND YOUTUBER

SDI: STRATEGIC DEFENSE INITIATIVE
FORMAT: AMSTRAD CPC
YEAR OF RELEASE: 1989
DEVELOPER: SOURCE SOFTWARE LTD
PUBLISHER: ACTIVISION
ORIGINAL PRICE: 9.99 POUNDS

BACK IN THE '80s, pocket money was very limited – a few pence a week besides a couple of 10p pieces for the arcade. This encouraged me to play as well as possible to extend those arcade experiences, but that short session was never enough and I always wanted to play those games at home. After weeks or even months of saving, I would eventually be able to buy a new game, usually at Woolworths or WHSmith. On one occasion I was lucky to be taken to Hamleys toy shop in London. On the top floor they featured an amazing selection of all of the latest computer games,

and it was there that I saw SDI: Strategic Defense Initiative for the Amstrad for the first time. Wow, the excitement! The box art and screenshots looked amazing. OK, they were screen shots from various formats, but surely the Amstrad version couldn't look too bad? I spent my hard-earned savings and couldn't wait to get home and indulge in hours of Star Wars Defense System action!

I waited for the 20 minutes loading time with building excitement. The loading screen wasn't all that impressive: as the lines came across and built the picture piece by piece, it looked limited colourwise. But no fear, I knew the game was going to be amazing. As I played my first game, however, the shock of disappointment washed over me. No in-game music, poor audio and only a single blue colour used in the entire game. And to top it off, it played super slowly with a terrible frame rate. Everything that I loved about the arcade was gone. Instead it felt like an empty shell.

It was horrible. I'd spent all of my pocket money and was left with a game that wasn't worth playing. If you grew up and played computer games in the '80s, "screenshots from various formats" is a phrase you'll be familiar with. They usually displayed the arcade, Amiga and Atari ST versions on the back. But every now and again they would feature shots from at least the Commodore 64 or Amstrad CPC versions. I felt like I had been completely misled, as it was effectively a conversion of the ZX Spectrum release and not the arcade at all.

I was determined not to be fooled again. From that point forward I was more selective, and if I didn't like a game or if it wasn't as represented on the back of the box, then I would take it back. I also stopped buying a lot of budget software and instead focused on the bigger names even if it meant taking longer to save. With that approach I eventually saved enough to buy Domark's Star Wars Trilogy box set – now that was awesome!

Alan can be found on Twitter at @VVVGamer

FACT! *Amstrad Action* magazine really liked SDI, awarding it 82%. Even though it plays like a particularly dull dog. The 49% given by *Amstrad Computer User* makes more sense.

BIONIC GRANNY

BY

-MASTERTRONIC-

ITS NEARLY FOUR O'CLOCK AND TIME FOR THE
KIDS TO COME HOME FROM SCHOOL.

YOU'R A BIONIC GRANNY AND ARE WAITING
OUTSIDE THE SCHOOL TO HIT THE KIDS AS
LEAVE.

SOME WILL WALK DOWN THE ROADS BUT OTHERS
WILL TRY TO EVADE YOU BY KEEPING OFF THE
ROADS.

DON'T LET THE LOLLIPOP LADY THROW
LOLLIPOPS AT YOU.

PRESS A KEY TO CONTINUE

BIONIC GRANNY

FORMAT: COMMODORE 64
YEAR OF RELEASE: 1984
DEVELOPER: UNKNOWN
PUBLISHER: MASTERTRONIC
ORIGINAL PRICE: 1.99 POUNDS

Terrifying skull-faced goons hang out near the school as Bionic Granny goes for the frog-headed child on the right.

FOR YEARS I THOUGHT that this game was made to cash in on the popularity of *Super Gran*, a TV series about an elderly Scottish lady who receives super powers. However, it actually predates the show! It seems that unnaturally beefed-up grandmothers were just a popular idea in the mid-eighties.

The cassette inlay describes the titular Granny as lurking outside a school at home time, trying to "zap" children with her laser-powered umbrella. It describes the aim of the game as "Run for your life before she gets you too!" which is nonsense since you actually play as her. It's not a good sign when the people writing the game's description don't know anything about it.

More pertinent instructions are given on the game's title screen, but it is so full of grammatical and typographical errors that it would make a middle school English teacher faint. But the aim is clear: you are Bionic Granny, and you must assault as many children as possible. They never say how Granny came to have parts of her body replaced with cybernetic equivalents or why she is compelled to physically injure kids. That's a shame as I'm sure it would be a fascinating and tragic story. I'll have to wait for a novelisation.

On starting the game, you're presented with a road system leading into a school at the top of the screen. A giant clock floating in the air shows the time as four o'clock. Then, children run out of the school and down the screen. Either the scale or

SCORE 000000   LIVES 2   HI 005275

Granny appears to be firing a rifle in the air, but she is actually just waving a stick.

perspective is insane – the entire school building is the same width as the road, and the children leaving the school are as big as a quarter of a football pitch.

Bionic Granny herself is stuck at the bottom of the screen, only capable of moving left and right. She has two frames of animation and no leg movement, so she appears to glide around on roller skates. She constantly waves a wooden stick in the air, presumably having lost her laser-powered brolly.

So you can only move left and right, trying to crash into the school kids as they attempt to run off the bottom of the screen. If any touch you, they instantly disappear and points are earned.

But you do not stand unopposed in your quest to violently assail innocent youngsters who cannot fight back. The lollipop lady, who has sworn to use her crossing guard powers to stop Bionic Granny, frantically runs around the screen firing stop signs from her infinite supply. This may be possible due to magical powers or futuristic technology – she appears to be the offspring of Skeletor and one of the aliens from *Close Encounters of the Third Kind*, so she probably has access to both.

And... that's it. You just slide around horizontally, trying to avoid the lollipop lady's projectiles and smack as many kids as possible into oblivion. Not only is it mind-meltingly dull, it is also annoying – the stop

37

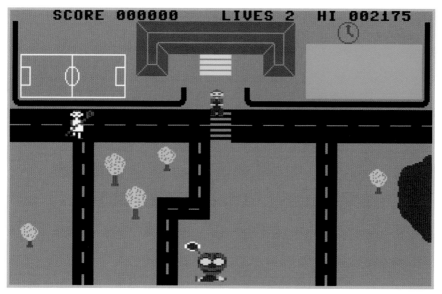

Oddly, a giant red face appears when Granny dies. Perhaps it's her soul escaping in the form of a demonic terminator skull.

signs launched by the lollipop lady move at a terrifying speed and are almost impossible to dodge if you're directly under them. Eventually, your score gets near 5,000 and the supply of kids dries up, leaving only one that runs down the right-hand side of the screen. Breach the 5,000 point barrier and you reach level 2 – which is exactly the same as level 1. The fun never starts with *Bionic Granny*!

The sound consists of two audio annoyances: a jolly, twinkly tune that plays constantly in the background

The game's cast: Bionic Granny, lollipop lady, school girl, school boy, school girl 2, school boy 2. Wonderful.

and an odd noise like a rubber band being pinged against a damp towel that pipes up when you injure a child. Earplugs are recommended.

Bionic Granny is utter, utter tosh. Even for the budget price of £1.99 (about £6 today, taking into account inflation), there's no excuse for such half-baked nonsense. Well, I say half-baked, but frankly this game isn't even one-fifth-baked. It's become infamous in the Commodore 64 community, to the extent that it spawned an enhanced – and differently spelled – remake in 2010 called *Bionik Granny Returns*.

The publisher Mastertronic was incredibly prolific, releasing well over 100 games for the Commodore 64. But the actual developers of *Bionic Granny* remain uncredited and unknown. It's possible, however, that it was written by brothers David and Richard Darling. *Bionic Granny* was put together using Mirrorsoft's "The Games Creator", an easy-to-use construction kit that required no programming experience but imposed heavy limitations on any game made with it. The Darlings themselves actually made "The Games Creator", and they used it to produce several substandard games for Mastertronic such as *BMX Racers* and *Mind Control*. The text on their title screens often included grammatical errors, too. But they went on to found the very successful company Codemasters

The game's cover art has a truly terrifying face in the background, like a mummified John Lennon.

REVIEW SCORES

Commodore User magazine's weird scoring system gave *Bionic Granny* 6 points out of a potential 20, which is at least 4 too many.

OTHER VERSIONS

Some online sources mention an Amstrad CPC version – I am very pleased to announce that it doesn't seem to exist. Nice to end on a positive note. Continuing the genre of overpowered pensioners, TV's *Super Gran* had its own rubbish game released in 1985.

that still publishes hit games to this day, so even if they did make *Bionic Granny*, I think we can all collectively forgive them.

CAR — RACE

→ KEY-PLAY

JOY-PLAY

PUSH ↑ OR ↓ KEY

AND

SPACE

CAR
RACE

SCORE
00000m

HI-SCORE
00000m

FUEL
1000

© AMPLE

CAR RACE

FORMAT: MSX1
YEAR OF RELEASE: 1983
DEVELOPER: AMPLE SOFTWARE / PANASONIC
PUBLISHER: AMPLE SOFTWARE
ORIGINAL PRICE: APPROX. 13 POUNDS

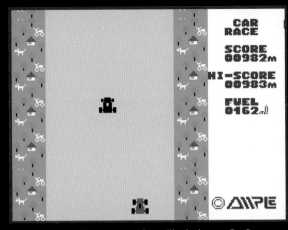

Red car goes up, black car goes down. That's the way Car Race goes.

NO MESSING ABOUT with the title here – you know exactly what you're getting. It's like calling the latest FIFA game "Ball Kick" or calling *Bioshock* "Weirdo Shoot". Except it isn't really a race at all, meaning half of the title is actually inaccurate.

Clearly inspired by the arcade game *Bump 'n' Jump*, *Car Race* (or *Car-Race* as it appears in the game) actually involves driving at a high speed down an infinitely long, entirely straight road until you run out of fuel. It's a bit like

a nightmare induced by driving on a German autobahn for too long.

First impressions are that it's a fairly basic affair. The title screen is entirely text-based, and a jolly but repetitive tune plays in the background. Sadly things do not become more sophisticated when you play the game.

The graphics are about as primitive as they can be before you can't tell what they are. The road you race down is entirely blank, and at the sides there is a continual loop of infinite dogs, trees, huts and bicycles. It feels like the game was written in a weekend. Worst of all is the audio, which is a constant, horrible whining sound that's presumably supposed to represent your engine noise. After a few seconds, it feels like there are drugged bees trapped in both your ears.

Your first game of *Car Race* will inevitably proceed as follows:

You press the space bar to start.

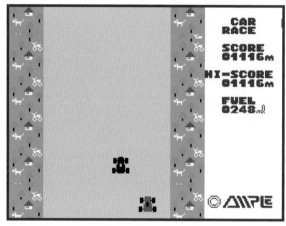

A road that stretches on forever through an infinitely repeating suburb. This is purgatory.

You take in what's on the screen – your car is at the bottom and a straight road leads upwards. A black car is swerving towards you.

You hold down space to accelerate.

The "Game Over" screen appears within five seconds of starting.

You are extremely confused.

The reason for the game ending is that you've run out of fuel, despite your score telling you that you've only travelled about 80 metres. This is because the way *Car Race* deals with fuel is utterly bonkers – you burn more petrol the slower you go. At the minimum speed your car starts at, the entire tank empties in about 3.5 seconds. The instant the game starts, you have to hold down the space bar and never release it – and even then your 1,000 units of fuel will have reduced to about 350 by the time you get up to speed!

So, you've worked out how to actually play the game for more than a few seconds and discovered just how barebones it is. Then, black cars appear at the top of the screen, weaving down towards you. There is always exactly one of these cars on the screen at all times. Your car moves left and right quite slowly, and the enemy vehicles are a lot faster – some of them swerve all over the screen at an insane speed, making them effectively impossible

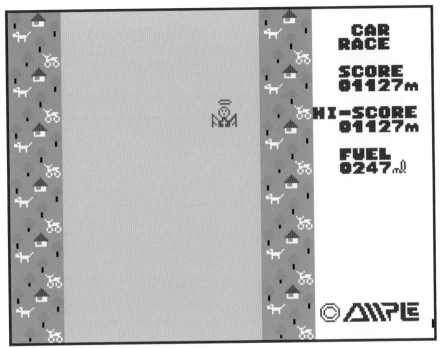

When you crash, the top half of an angel flies off up the road. Although it could be an alien chasing an inner tube.

to avoid. Collision with one of them makes your car explode and costs you 100 units of fuel, but your car is immediately replaced by one moving at the speed you were last travelling at.

Your ever-diminishing fuel supply

can be replenished by running over tiny blue petrol pumps that randomly appear in the road, granting you an extra 100 units. Tragically, they fly down the screen so fast that you can't possibly move over to them in time; you have to hope they will appear pretty much directly in front of you.

And that is all of *Car Race*'s gameplay. Hold down accelerate and never let go for a second or your fuel evaporates faster than a drop of water on a lightsaber. Shuffle left and right, hoping that a fuel pickup appears in a favourable position and the next black car isn't one of the crazy, swerving ones. The best strategy by far is to move over to the far right of the screen and swerve carefully, as the enemies mostly stay on the left and fuel often appears on the right. By a combination of this and saint-like patience, you can reach the maximum score of 65,535 metres after about 20 solid minutes of mind-numbingly tedious play.

Car Race's biggest sin is that of wasted opportunity. The movement and scrolling are smooth and the collision detection is solid. If they'd actually put some time and thought into the

Here's a low-quality picture of the cover art, because the screenshots are all the same.

game design, it could be quite good fun. But sadly, it's just a bleak lump of nothing that's so dull you could fall asleep playing it – if the horrifying engine noise didn't keep you awake.

Ample Software released two other games: a bizarre alcoholism-based platformer called *Super Drinker* and *Scramble Eggs*, a rubbish, simplified version of *Scramble* where the enemy spaceships are replaced with eggs. Yes, really.

REVIEW SCORES
None known

OTHER VERSIONS
None, but you can play *Bump 'n' Jump* (AKA *Burnin' Rubber*) on various systems, and it's pretty much the same game but a million times better.

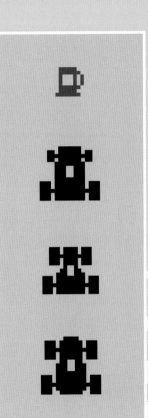

COUNT DUCKULA 2

FORMAT: AMSTRAD CPC
YEAR OF RELEASE: 1992
DEVELOPER: UNKNOWN
PUBLISHER: ALTERNATIVE SOFTWARE
ORIGINAL PRICE: 3.99 POUNDS

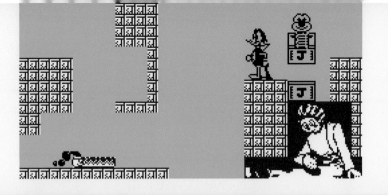

This screen appears to feature a fresco of Raggedy Ann after being stabbed in the stomach.

THE AMSTRAD CPC suffered from a horrible plague throughout its lifespan that affected many of the games released for it. It was a particularly insidious disease known as Lazy ZX Spectrum Conversions. The only cure was an injection of money and time from game publishers, and as you're probably aware from the contents of this book, that medication was in extremely short supply.

The Amstrad is capable of displaying a low resolution mode with 16 colours, similar to the Commodore 64 but with a larger potential palette and more vivid hues. But it can also produce a higher resolution screen similar to the Spectrum, albeit with only

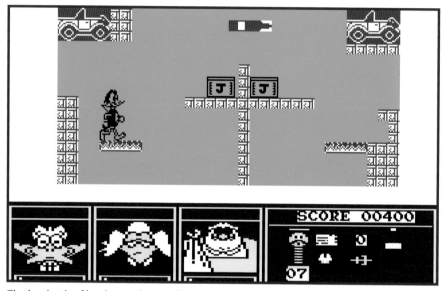

That's a bottle of ketchup at the top of the screen. Yes, really.

four colours at once. It also shares the same processor which led to developers realising they could just port over the code of a Spectrum game in a few days. It would have fewer colours than the original version and run much slower, as the graphics were converted to the exact Amstrad format in real time. But some companies simply didn't care – the Spectrum had a much bigger market share in the UK so the Amstrad versions were treated as an afterthought. That didn't stop them charging the same money for them though...

Count Duckula 2 is one of the very

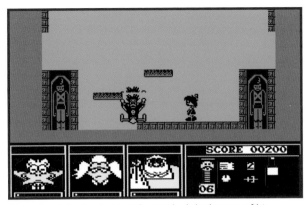

Count Duckula dies because he touched the bottom of his screen. His hair is duplicated due to hideous graphical errors.

apparently because he doesn't like cute things. Fair enough.

Things start off well with a colourful and nicely drawn loading screen that leads into a funky remix of the cartoon's title music. Then things fall off a cliff faster than Wile E. Coyote strapped to Acme's finest rocket-powered anvil.

The graphics are absolutely dreadful. A pixelated mess representing Duckula stands in a mostly empty screen peppered with ugly blocks that look like they've escaped from a 1982 magazine type-in. Occasionally there are large images of toys in the corners, but they've been reduced to two colours without being redrawn and are a total mess as a result.

Then the graphics move and the true horror begins. Everything is jerky and flickery beyond belief – the top of Duckula's head seems to be detached

worst examples of a lazy conversion. And as the game is distressingly poor in the first place, Alternative Software took something dreadful and made it into something frankly unholy.

The second game to be based on the popular children's cartoon from British animation studio Cosgrove Hall, *Count Duckula 2* follows the exploits of the vegetarian vampire duck as he gets stranded on Planet Cute. The entire world is covered with animated toys whose touch slowly kills our hero,

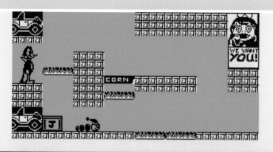

According to the instructions, the thing saying "CORN" is the torn-off top of a cereal packet. Even the items you collect are things you'd find in a bin.

from the rest of his body as he shuffles and twitches across the platforms. There is no jumping animation, meaning he takes Aled Jones' advice and just walks in the air. The enemies feature minimal animation. Everything runs like it's being updated in real-time by a tranquilised sloth in a bath of treacle. Sound is limited to a handful of beepy spot effects.

The game is based primarily around waiting for constantly moving plat-forms to be in the correct place to allow you to prog-ress. And when I say "moving" I actually mean "flickering in and out of existence at different points on the screen". As the game runs at half the speed it was designed for, you spend an awful lot of time waiting. The evil toys that sap your strength can be stunned with your ketchup gun, except for the jack-in-the-boxes which can't be shot or avoided.

Beyond the stiflingly tedious game design lie even more technical problems. The controls are painfully unresponsive, with a lag of around half a second between you pressing a button and something actually happening. You frequently merge into the corners of platforms as you try and jump on them. And there's yet another massive problem caused

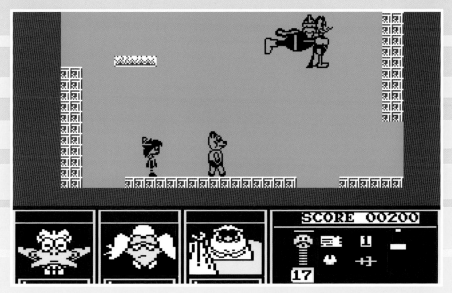

Tremendous Terrence helpfully provides a way to avoid a game-crippling programming oversight.

by the lazy conversion from the Spectrum original...

For some reason the Amstrad version stops you jumping off the top of the screen. If you try, Duckula bangs his head and plummets straight down. As the levels were designed assuming you would have this ability, this oversight causes multiple problems. The most serious is that the second screen is impossible to complete by standard means, as any attempt to reach the moving platforms leads to falling off the bottom of the screen and instant death. The only way to progress is to call Tremendous Terrence, a superhero who carries you to the next screen. You can only use

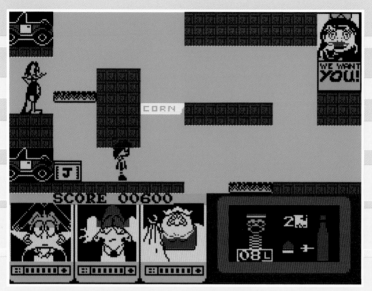

The Spectrum version. Still dreadful... just less dreadful.

this level skip every so often, so it's a kick in the teeth to be forced to use it on screen two, especially since you will need him on the very next screen when you inevitably get your head stuck in the ceiling.

Count Duckula 2 is an absolute travesty. Amstrad owners deserved better than lazy Spectrum ports, and the people who paid money for the game – possibly on the strength of the first *Count Duckula* title – certainly deserved better than this digital farce.

The people responsible for producing this dreadful conversion remain unknown as they understandably didn't put their names on it anywhere. Alternative Software released dozens of budget games for the Amstrad, including multiple children's television tie-ins like *Postman Pat* and *Fireman Sam*. They also spewed out the nightmarishly dreadful *BMX Ninja* and *Rik the Roadie*, and as such are still considered beyond redemption to this day.

REVIEW SCORES

Amstrad Action felt that 3% was a fair score, and I can't disagree.

OTHER VERSIONS

Spectrum: As previously mentioned, the original version is effectively the same game except it works properly and there's no sound. The graphics are far more colourful, the crippling bugs aren't present, and it runs literally twice as fast. However it's still an utterly atrocious game – in fact, in 1993 the readers of Your Sinclair magazine voted it the worst Spectrum game of all time by a landslide. (Clearly they had never tried to play *SQIJ!*)

Commodore 64: This version had a lot more effort put into it and is far superior in every respect as a result. It even has an extra shoot 'em up section at the start. It's not great by any means, but it's the best version by a country mile.

THE MOST DISAPPOINTING GAME I EVER BOUGHT

BY JEFF MINTER,
GAME CODER AND FOUNDER
OF LLAMASOFT):-D

ASTEROIDS
FORMAT: COMMODORE VIC-20
YEAR OF RELEASE: 1983
DEVELOPER: S. MUNNERY
PUBLISHER: BUG-BYTE
ORIGINAL PRICE: 7.00 POUNDS

THINK ABOUT THE defining characteristics of the coin-op Asteroids: *precise, smoothly-animated gameplay that was extremely challenging but ultimately fair; sparsely beautiful and pure vector graphics; simple but effective audio that served to ramp up the tension. Now imagine something with characteristics the diametric opposite of those, and you have* Asteroids *by S. Munnery. Tiny character mode "asteroids" lurched around the screen in giant character-grid-quantised steps. Occasionally, the game would begin with one of them placed directly on top of your ship, killing you instantly. Your ship was a strange kind of horseshoe-shaped thing that would trundle around the screen forlornly making noises like a Hoover, and when you pressed the FIRE button, a line of full stops would come out of its nose.*

It was a complete and utter pile of smeg, and for me, it was one of the final straws that broke the dromedary and convinced me to start Llamasoft. I believe my thinking on the matter was along the lines of "For fuck's sake, even I could do better than that." Inspired, I founded Llamasoft and made a completely shit version of Defender

for the Vic-20. I did go on to do some other slightly less shit things later on though.

Playing this game felt like being repeatedly stabbed in the eyes with recently sharpened pencils whilst being comprehensively kneed in the bollocks by Margaret Thatcher. S. Munnery did do another game called Cosmiads on the Vic-20 years later; it was actually marginally less terrible than Asteroids and only made you feel like flushing your own head down the toilet.

Buying Asteroids made me a bit wary of buying games from software houses that sold a bunch of games by different authors. I'd bought a game off Bug-Byte before that hadn't been entirely dreadful, and it was on the strength of that

experience that I ponied up seven whole Earth quid for that traumatising Asteroids. There was a lot of a "buy any old crap from shitty programmers and shove it out there because people will buy anything" attitude that a lot of early software houses succumbed to in those days, and this was just Bug-Byte doing that, I suppose. I think that's why Llamasoft ended up being such a one man band in the end. I may have made shitty games myself in the early days, but at least I actively tried to get better at it instead of just selling any old crap because I could get away with it.

Jeff can be found on Twitter at @llamasoft_ox – follow him for Sheep Time on Periscope.

FACT!

S. Munnery is Simon Munnery, who went on to have an extremely successful career in comedy, performing stand-up and writing for TV and radio.

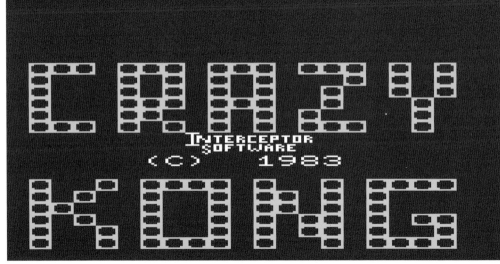

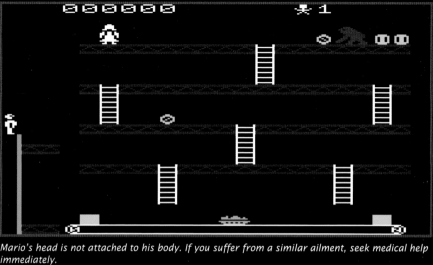

Mario's head is not attached to his body. If you suffer from a similar ailment, seek medical help immediately.

ALONG WITH *PAC-MAN*, *Donkey Kong* was a cultural phenomenon in the early 80s, and every home computer had multiple unlicensed clones made for it. Sadly, most of them were pretty rubbish, and Interceptor's *Crazy Kong* is certainly no exception.

The usual set-up applies – an oversized gorilla has kidnapped your girlfriend for some reason, and to rescue her you have to climb up some

gantries whilst the ape throws barrels at you. The instructions even specifically call the main character Mario. Copyright was not well-respected at the time, to say the least.

Things start badly with an ugly title picture that isn't centred in the middle of the screen and offers no discernible way to start the game. Tragically the game does start up after a while, and your buyer's remorse really kicks in.

According to Interceptor's mail-order advert for *Crazy Kong*, it "includes some of the best graphics ever seen on the VIC-20". I'm not sure where they're hidden, as all the ones actually displayed on screen would be better described as "adequate". Kong himself is a purple sloth. Mario's girlfriend is a ghost with a bell on her head. The row of blue boats at the bottom of the screen are supposed to be custard pies. And when Mario dies, he turns into a green angel that looks more like some kind of monster from a 50s B movie.

Animation is almost absent – things jerk around the screen, and Mario just flicks one leg out behind himself when he's not standing still. The jumping animation is bizarre – Mario slowly hovers into the air, floats forward one character space and lands. Sound is limited entirely to an annoying beep every time you move and a weird laser gun effect every time you jump.

The very first thing you have to do in *Crazy Kong* is extremely frustrating. You have to walk onto a constantly falling platform just as it teleports back into its starting position – an irritating leap of faith that takes several games to get the hang of. One wrong move and you fall to your death, or you glitch into the conveyor belt below, which forces you to kill yourself by touching one of the deadly yellow blocks. The lethargic controls do not to help.

The rest of the level involves jumping over the bright blue pies, which is extremely easy, then dodging the barrels as you make your way to the top. There are no hammers with which to smash the barrels in this version, so you rely entirely on timing your movements and jumping. The barrels alternate between two different paths, so it doesn't take long to figure out an optimum route. The only real threat are the controls, which will occasionally leave you stuck on a ladder when a barrel's coming your way. Oddly, Mario moves faster the closer he gets to the top of the screen; by the time he's reached the third girder, he's zipping around like a coffee-addled businessman on a supercharged Segway.

So you reach Mario's phantasmic,

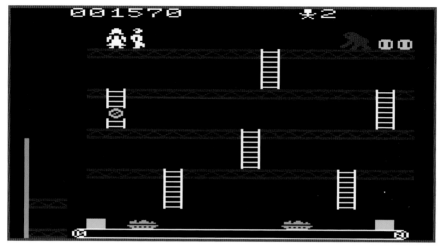

Mario is victorious! Sloth Kong could just run up and punch him, but instead he stays close to his comforting barrels.

bell-headed sweetheart and the level ends! You are awarded some points and... that's it. The same level starts again, just running slightly faster. As you can easily get to the top in 30 seconds, there's a serious lack of variety and value for money. Eventually it gets too fast to actually complete, or at least it seemed that way to me after playing it for far, far too long.

Crazy Kong is one of the worst examples of an early eighties *Donkey Kong* rip-off, and that's saying something. The graphics are actually better than some other attempts (yes, really!) but everything else conspires to remove any rational reason to play it. It's a buggy, fiddly, annoying mess with almost nothing to it. It's still better than C-Tech's infamous *Krazy*

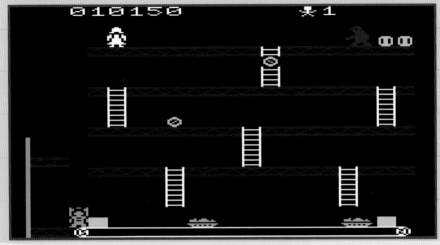

On death, Mario apparently transforms into the X-Men villain Sauron.

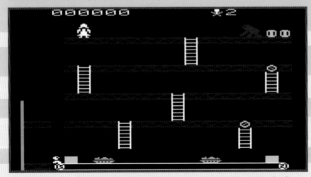

Our hero gets stuck in the floor. Tragically, his only method of escape is to gnaw his own legs off.

INTERCEPTOR
SOFTWARE

CRAZY KONG

SUITABLE FOR THE UNEXPANDED
VIC 20

WRITTEN IN MACHINE CODE

The box art is terrifying. If this was the cover of a VHS tape, I would have rented it without question.

Fun Factory labels. Whilst there were some absolute stinkers amongst their early games, the quality increased hugely as time progressed.

Kong for the Spectrum, but then so is having explosive diarrhoea on a long train journey.

Interceptor published a huge number of games in the 80s and early 90s, both under their own name and the Players, Players Premier, Pandora and

REVIEW SCORES

Computer and Video Games magazine described the game as having "more bugs than a flea-bitten moggy". Yet somehow they gave it 6/10 for both value and playability! They misspelled the name as Krazy Kong and claimed the game cost 95p more than it did, so perhaps they were distracted by a particularly impressive dance routine at the time.

OTHER VERSIONS

Commodore 64: Pleasingly, this version is totally different. It has appalling graphics and is brutally difficult, but it is far more fun to play than the VIC-20 version.

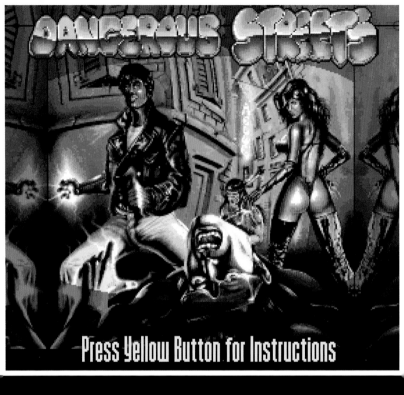

Press Yellow Button for Instructions

DANGEROUS STREETS

FORMAT: COMMODORE AMIGA CD32
YEAR OF RELEASE: 1993
DEVELOPER: MICROMANIA SOFTWARE
PUBLISHER: FLAIR
ORIGINAL PRICE: 25.99 POUNDS

PLAYER SELECT!

From left to right, top to bottom we have: Sgiosa Capeli (works in a disco), Pinen (lorry driver), Tony (playboy), Luisa (gym teacher), Macalosh (spiritual boss of the Sioux), Ombra (expert palmist), Keo (custodian for an old castle), Lola (top model)

IGNITED BY THE home release of *Street Fighter II* the previous year, the market for fighting games was huge in 1993. The Amiga had few exclusives to call its own – the only one of note was *Body Blows*, a fairly simple affair with nice graphics. A really solid fighter would be a license to print money, surely? It seems that Micromania Software certainly thought so, but they somehow replaced the word

"solid" with "unplayable" in their design documents.

The characters in *Dangerous Streets* are an odd bunch even for a fighting game. They have a very 70s vibe to their designs, and they mostly seem to be refugees from an Italian disco of that era, with the inexplicable exception of a blue monk who has springs strapped to his feet. The two female characters both wear stripper outfits

Macalosh has some kind of bowel problem whilst Keo struggles with his foot springs.

impressive, because as soon as you see the characters move, any prettiness flies out of the window with a speed that would startle a cheetah on steroids.

The animation is beyond laughable, to the extent that you begin to wonder if the movements were designed by a primitive computer that had human motion explained to it by a semi-comatose drunkard. The characters jerk and twitch like a low-budget zombie movie that has half its frames missing. A particular favourite is the way Luisa's head twitches alarmingly as she walks, making it seem like she is auditioning for an especially disturbing remake of *The Exorcist*. And Macalosh's standing pose manages to look ridiculous through using only two frames of animation – he half-squats

so skimpy you wouldn't let your kids play the game.

One of the most notable things about *Dangerous Streets* is that it looks quite pretty in screenshots. The characters are competently drawn and well-defined, and the backgrounds are colourful. This was possibly a marketing strategy to make magazine reviews and the back of the box more

Top five ridiculous moves! Slab defence, large cap shield, hair gel attack, scalp lash, and mini man attack.

at a gravity defying angle as if he is trying to defecate in an invisible toilet without his arse cheeks touching the seat.

The fighting moves that the characters use are worse still. They're an almost animation-free cavalcade of seemingly random, jerky attacks with no thought put into how they would affect the gameplay. Each character has several ridiculous, wannabe-comedic moves that only further ruin any potential fun: Lola can fire lumps of hair gel out of her hair. Tony can project a small, blue demon from his fingertips to hide behind. Pinen has a hollow chest cavity which opens up to reveal a tiny version of himself that flies along the screen, fists pummelling. Macalosh tries to whip his hair into his opponent's eyes and can turn into a monster so ill-defined that I have no idea what it's supposed to be. Keo can summon a squid to protect himself, whilst Luisa's defence involves turning into a solid block of metal. Sgiosa can make his hideous, fluorescent catsuit glow, which apparently protects him. Ombra somehow dives into the floor and flies back out again further along the screen, a protracted move which actually counts as his forward jump so he does it all the bloody time.

I can only assume that the game designers were trying to make things light-hearted and tongue-in-cheek. But for that to work, it needs to be backed

Macalosh has turned into a thing. Possibly the offspring of a panther and a gorilla?

up by charm and wit and not be one of the worst fighting games ever commercially released.

The sound is equally poor. Dull, bleeping Euro disco tracks are streamed from the CD for background music. The contact sound effects only seem to kick in if they feel like it, and some of them are just blasts of white noise. Or possibly the game just blasts white noise every so often, I can't tell. Worst of all are the pre-fight announcements of the characters' names, all of which sound like they were recorded from people shouting across a bathroom into a dodgy microphone.

But as bad as the audio-visual horror gets, it's the gameplay that really plumbs the depths of incompetence. Fighting games need to be carefully balanced with tight controls and clear feedback at all times. *Dangerous Streets* eschews these things in favour of a man who blows into his hat so it expands to giant size and he can hide behind it.

I will now attempt to explain what it's like to play *Dangerous Streets* without resorting to sexual swearwords. Firstly, the controls make no sense. Some of the four face buttons on the horrible CD32 control pad duplicate each other, but not all the time. Moving your character across the screen quickly is a nightmare due to the bizarre jump animations that most characters have. Hit detection is a

It also gives you instructions on how to load the game after you have loaded the game.

Luisa versus Luisa. Can you tell which is which? No? Neither can the players.

joke, and characters don't always react to being hit – add in the almost random sound effects, and most of the time you have no idea if you've actually landed a blow on your opponent. Each character's limited "super-move" is far less effective than his or her standard forward attack. Characters can move slightly off-screen so you can't see them. If both players select the same character, they look identical and there is no way to tell them apart. There is no sense of weight to any of the fighters, and it feels as if you have very little influence over what they do – unless you just hold down one button... you can beat the computer by holding down one button.

Dangerous Streets is an utter travesty. A twitchy, jerking mess far worse than even the infamous fighting game failures *Shaq Fu* and *Rise of the Robots*. The CD32 hadn't been out for long and you might think Commodore would want to keep this garbage as far away from their new console as possible before people compared it to *Street Fighter II* and bought a Super Nintendo. Instead they included the game with all new CD32s and named the resulting bundle the *Dangerous Streets* pack. I am not making this up.

Commodore had made several questionable business decisions over the years, but this was possibly their most ridiculous. It, of course, did nothing to help sales. After a slew of legal problems and component supply failures, Commodore declared bankruptcy in April 1994 and the Amiga CD32 went off sale only eight months after its release. It was never released in North America.

Developer Micromania were never heard of before or after *Dangerous Streets*, which is in itself a beautiful mercy. Publisher Flair were responsible for various other CD32 pack-in games and also the execrable *Surf Ninjas* – an Amiga CD32 exclusive that is so bad the only reason I haven't covered it in this book is because I wrote so much about *Dangerous Streets*.

REVIEW SCORES

Amiga Power awarded the game 3%. As in three out of a hundred. At the time I assumed the score was comically low as some kind of protest against substandard games having entire console bundle packs named after them. Then a few months later, I attempted to play it and realised they were entirely serious.

The One magazine gave it 22% and described it as a "freshly laid turd". German magazine *Amiga Joker* somehow decided it was worth a frighteningly inflated 44%, despite utterly eviscerating the gameplay in their review. But they thought the graphics and sound were good so they may have been mentally incapacitated by paint fumes or something.

OTHER VERSIONS

Commodore Amiga 1200 (AGA): This version is extremely similar, as internally the CD32 is essentially an A1200 with an extra chip in the graphics architecture to help take advantage of the added CD drive. However, without said CD drive, the music is reduced to slightly discordant *Street Fighter II*-style tunes and the loading takes forever. What's more, it comes on three disks so you have to keep swapping them. As a result it's actually worse than the CD32 version.

Commodore Amiga 500/500+/600 (OCS/ECS): Amazingly, this version is worse still! The lesser power of the older Amiga models led to smaller game characters, less colourful backgrounds and no in-game music at all. Even *Amiga Joker* couldn't stomach this version, which they blessed with a 20% rating as it flew into their rubbish bin.

The Amiga 500/500+/600 version, with smaller fighters and less colours, but all the perverse costumes!

PC: A rare PC port of an Amiga game! If only it were rarer. The fighters in this version are huge and far more detailed, and if both players select the same character they are actually different colours. But the good news ends there. It is horribly sluggish on the hardware of the time and the soundtrack consists entirely of lifeless jangly music. For reasons I cannot begin to fathom, huge foreground items were added to each stage, obscuring about a third of the screen.

GRAFFITI MAN

FORMAT: ATARI ST
YEAR OF RELEASE: 1987
DEVELOPER: RELINE
PUBLISHER: RAINBOW ARTS
ORIGINAL PRICE: 24.99 POUNDS

THE GAME STARTS. The screen is filled with grotesquely ugly freaks jerking around everywhere. You move your character slightly, and he apparently touches a freak, despite clearly not being close enough. He instantly explodes in a mess of blood. You lose a life and respawn at the start. You try to move carefully along the screen, but attempting to move vertically in the play area means you can't tell exactly where your character is. He gets near a freak and explodes again. You are now on your last life. You manage to navigate past the freaks for a few seconds then explode for no noticeable reason. The game is over. You have played *Graffiti Man* for less than 30 seconds, have lost all your lives, and have no idea what happened. You weep hot, bitter tears of anger and frustration.

Graffiti Man is a truly horrible game. The idea is to guide Mickey, "the multi-talented Graffiti Man", across several locations so he can spray some paint on some walls. This will apparently enable him to join a famous graffiti gang. It's never made clear what Mickey's many talents are, but from the game we can assume they don't

Why is the road that colour? And why do the life counter men appear to have been boiled?

stretch to being able to see more than a few feet in front of his own nose or move at the speed of a normal human being.

The instant you start, you are thrown into a mess of sensory overload with a screen chock-full of caricatures on a hideous, orangey-brown background. It becomes obvious that you need to run from the left side of the screen to the right, dodging the various freakish stereotypes in your path. The playfield is split into three vertical planes that you can move between. The freaks, unable to change lanes, move horizontally from one side of the screen to the other, looping back round when they disappear

The bearded man releases tiny clockwork spies from a cardboard box. It's a hobby, I suppose.

off the edge. It sounds simple, and it absolutely is simple. But one thing it is not is easy.

As previously described, your first game of *Graffiti Man* is likely to last only a few confusing seconds. There is stuff everywhere and it all kills you instantly. But it is only when you understand how things work that the true horror begins.

The game chugs along, usually around a painfully slow six frames a second, meaning our hero Mickey walks in slow motion as if in a bad dream. This also makes the fast-paced enemy freaks jerk around in an astonishingly ugly manner. The controls are painfully unresponsive, meaning quick reactions to onscreen events are impossible, and it's very difficult to stop on the middle plane. When you reach the right-hand side of the screen, it begins to scroll with very little space in front of Mickey, meaning that freaks can appear and kill you before you can possibly react. Coupled with the dodgy collision detection, the only way to proceed is to predict the behaviour of the looping enemies like some kind of freak-obsessed sociologist.

So! You are now the world's leading expert in predicting freak movement patterns and getting an unresponsive, slow-motion graffiti artist to navigate them. What else do you need to look out for? How about the super-fast projectiles that some enemies fire at random and will kill you if they get anywhere near you? How about the way you can outrun the screen scrolls on level 3 and disappear off into the digital ether? How about the small objects that fire diagonally across the screen and are almost impossible to dodge in certain positions? How about the fact that Mickey can jump and duck, but that both moves are completely useless? How about the way these problems make the game so frustrating that you may furiously punch through the TV connected to your Atari ST? Master all of these and you may make it through all four levels!

Top row: Freakishly ugly roller skater, dangerously barefoot skateboarder, Steve Martin in Roxanne, blatantly racist caricature. Bottom row: Crazy octopus, constantly punching sailor, creepy spy cliché, inexplicable shears-wielding spy.

You start off in a street full of punks and pensioners, move on to a train station full of psychotic porters, pass through some docks filled with deadly sailors and wildlife, and then finally graduate to what appears to be the lawn of the White House covered with spies and dogs. I don't know what part of Washington, DC, Mickey lives in, but I think it's safe to assume the house prices are low and insurance costs are high.

Successfully completing a level leads to a bonus stage, but never has the word "bonus" been used more erroneously. You are presented with a piece of incredibly poor graffiti, such as a stick figure, and the game switches to mouse control to let you spray white pixels over it. The more of it you cover, the more points you get – the instructions say that you fail the bonus stage if you don't reach a certain score, but this is untrue. As there is no high score table, it's utterly pointless and dull. It also means that the pinnacle of Mickey's graffiti prowess is

Before and after Mickey's artistic endeavours. No wonder everyone wants to kill him.

likely event that you could make it through the four levels of frustrating dross, you would complete the entire game in well under eight minutes. The final insult is the price: an eye-watering £24.99.

But there are a few positives lying among the wreckage of *Graffiti Man*. The freakish caricature sprites are generally well drawn and amusing, and the animation of main character Mickey is excellent. The music is comprised of beepy-yet-funky little tunes that fit the game well, although the title theme is oddly bleak until the funk kicks in. And, most amazingly of all, there is actually a proper reward for beating the game! After the final bonus stage, you are treated to a very basic paint program that allows you to make your own crappy-looking graffiti and save it to a disk. That doesn't sound like much, but it's impressive for the time, considering the vast majority of games used to give you nothing more than a message saying "Congratulations!" for playing through them.

It's amazing to think that this rubbish was one of the first games re-

to make other people's crap childish drawings look even worse.

By this time you've probably worked out that purchasers of *Graffiti Man* wouldn't be very happy. Adding to their considerable buyers' remorse is the length of the game – each level takes less than a minute to complete, as does the bonus level. So in the un-

Presenting the horrible box art, where someone dressed a mannequin as Clint Ruin then badly airbrushed it!

leased by major publisher Rainbow Arts. It seems to be nothing more than a substandard port of the Amiga version that runs like a dog. Developers ReLINE somehow went on to make a game using the *Pink Panther* cartoon license as well as a semi-pornographic business management sim for the German market. It's hard to know which stigma was harder for them to bear: the creation of this game or the stupid capitalisation in their company name.

REVIEW SCORES
No known ST reviews, but in their review of the Amiga version, Australian Commodore and Amiga Review understandably said, "I didn't like this one at all!"

OTHER VERSIONS
Commodore Amiga: This superior version is far faster and smoother, running at double the frame rate, at least. As a result, the controls feel much more responsive, although the speed increase also means the entire game can be completed in less than five minutes.

Commodore 64: This 8-bit conversion also runs far more smoothly, although the graphics are featureless and drab. The scrolling is replaced with a flip-screen system that makes it possible for enemy freaks to seemingly appear out of nowhere and kill you instantly.

THE MOST DISAPPOINTING GAME I EVER BOUGHT

BY MENTSKI, BEARDED RETROSPECTIVE IDIOT AND OCCASIONAL FACE

OUT RUN
FORMAT: ZX SPECTRUM
YEAR OF RELEASE: 1987
DEVELOPER: PROBE SOFTWARE
PUBLISHER: U. S. GOLD
ORIGINAL PRICE: 8. 99 POUNDS
(12. 99 POUNDS FOR THE DISK)

*THE STORY has many layers...
where to begin?*

Let's start with a bit of founda-
tion: Back in those days there was
a concept that floated around the
schoolyard – the quest for the
"arcade-perfect" port. Now we all
know a Speccy conversion would
never be perfect, but we were
happy enough if it faithfully
recreated the gameplay.

In 1986, Elite released a conversion of Sega's Space Harrier,
seemingly doing the impossible and
creating a reasonably playable port
considering the hardware

limitations. We were suitably
impressed, and began to ask
questions. Converting Space Harrier
to the Speccy was considered
nigh-impossible; surely there's no
way you could ever squeeze Sega's
latest arcade hit, Out Run, into Sir
Clive's novelty doorstop?

Then some time in 1987 U.S.
Gold declared they'd acquired the
Out Run license and that it'd be
released for home computers in
time for Christmas.

The hype for this was huge. U.S.
Gold were attempting the impossible. Then we saw the screenshots

```
TIME 24        SCORE       188890
LAP   0" 55"" 1
```

184 km/h

STAGE 1

and our jaws dropped...

The Speccy screenshot showed the iconic Ferrari about to overtake a truck. The sprites were huge and looked like accurate representations of the arcade games graphics (albiet in monochrome of course, because ironically for a computer called the Spectrum, colour wasn't its strong point).

Maybe, just maybe, the programmers had been able to do what we all thought was impossible?

Release time came, and I remember rushing down to my local branch of Boots on a Saturday morning to get a copy. I finally had in my hands a copy of Out Run that I could play at home. On the back of the case were screenshots of the game on multiple formats, including the same shot for the Speccy that had made my mouth water in the magazines... This was it! The time had come!

Here's where it all turns for the worst: first up, the tape containing all the levels was accidentally recorded backwards.

On bringing the game home, I hurriedly loaded it only to find that I couldn't play it due to a bloody tape mastering error! I rushed back to Boots to get a replacement, only to find out all their Spectrum copies had the same error, and I'd have to wait three more days for new stock to arrive!

Three more days of sweaty anticipation. Three days of loading up the main program, staring at the menu, listening to the Speccy's beepy rendition of eminent background tune "Magical Sound Shower", waiting for a replacement copy so I could finally recreate the sheer joy I felt playing the greatest arcade game ever made.

Three days finally passed and I hurried to Boots after school to get my replacement copy. I know I said the time had come last time, but now I really mean it... The time had finally come!

Oh dear.

This was not the game they advertised. I mean, it looked similar, but it was clearly different. The giant sprites? Nowhere to be seen. Everything apart from the car had been shrunk by about 50%. The giant palm trees now looked more like roadside bonsai, and the towering trucks were now barely any taller than your Testarossa. The road was a pixellated, undefined mess... and worst of all was the speed.

Out Run on the ZX Spectrum is very, very slow. This game is supposed to be about driving a 180mph Ferrari through beautiful European-inspired locations. Playing this port made you wonder if you'd get there quicker if you got out and walked!

You'd think something like this would have been trashed in the press, but no! It got favourable reviews! Many said that despite its flaws, it was the best the Spectrum could have done... which was utter bunk too, as we found out shortly later when Ocean ported Chase H.Q. to riotous applause, blowing poor old Out Run out of the water in every possible way.

It was the first time I felt outright lied to by a games publisher. Those screenshots shown before release were pure fabrications (not just the Spectrum but shots for the Amstrad CPC and Atari ST, too!) A bond of trust was broken the day U.S. Gold lied about the quality of this game.

I also felt let down by the magazines of the day – not only for falling for U.S. Gold's propaganda, but for giving the game favourable reviews despite how bad it was and for not once questioning why the finished product didn't resemble the marketing bumpf. In time, older, cynical me would wonder if these magazines were on U.S. Gold's payroll.

Nearly 30 years on and we're still dealing with publisher lies and questioning journalistic integrity. The more things change, the more they stay the same.

And yet it didn't change my attitude to buying games. I still purchased appalling conversions of awesome arcade games for years. After all, it was the only way to play those games at home at the time.

Does anybody want a second-hand copy of *Street Fighter II* on Atari ST? Only played once...

Mentski can be found on YouTube at youtube.com/mentski and on Twitter at @mentski

FACT!

This is the infamously inaccurate screenshot, stitched together from two sources as tragically the high quality one was only partial. It was used for preview articles in *Your Sinclair*, *Sinclair User* and *Computer & Video Games* magazines as well as the back of the game box. There is no excuse.

BUTTON PRESS 3000

AN EXCLUSIVE, ORIGINAL TERRIBLE GAME
FOR YOU TO PLAY!

```
10 PRINT "PRESS T TO WIN"
20 PAUSE 0
30 IF INKEY$ ="t" THEN GO TO 70
40 IF INKEY$ ="T" THEN GO TO 70
50 IF INKEY$ ="c" THEN GO TO 80
60 CLS : PRINT "WRONG KEY, YOU LOSE": STOP
70 CLS : PRINT "WELL DONE, YOU WIN": STOP
80 CLS : PRINT "CHEAT MODE ACTIVE"
90 PRINT "PRESS T TO WIN"
100 PAUSE 0
110 GOTO 70
```

SIMPLY ENTER THIS PROGRAM INTO A SINCLAIR
ZX SPECTRUM AND RUN IT TO EXPERIENCE THE
DEAD-SOULED FRUSTRATION THAT ONLY COMES
FROM PLAYING A TRULY DREADFUL VIDEO GAME!

LOOK OUT FOR DETAILS ON HOW TO PRE-ORDER
THE BUTTON PRESS 3000 GAME OF THE YEAR
COLLECTOR'S EDITION AND DLC SEASON PASS!

© OCEAN 1986.

highlander

HIGHLANDER

FORMAT: ZX SPECTRUM
YEAR OF RELEASE: 1986
DEVELOPER: CANVAS
PUBLISHER: OCEAN
ORIGINAL PRICE: 7.95 POUNDS

HIGHLANDER IS WITHOUT doubt the best film ever made about an immortal Scotsman who only dies if you lop his head off. Unfortunately it spawned several awful sequels, none of which are worth the time it takes to watch them. But it's the 1986 home computer adaptation that takes the filthy, tarnished crown for being the worst of the franchise.

The *Highlander* game concentrates entirely on the sword fighting aspect of the film, pitting hero Connor MacLeod against three increasingly difficult opponents – friendly mentor Ramírez, creepy murderer Fizir (called Fasil in the film) and vicious maniac The Kurgen. Each opponent is loaded separately from the cassette tape, and you do not have to beat one to progress. This lack of continuity would be a shame if there was any joy to be had from playing the game at all.

On starting the game, the first thing to hit you is how incredibly ugly the characters are. MacLeod and his

You've been knocked over in the corner and will be hacked to bits. Get used to this.

opponents are nothing but a mess of big white blocks. They're decently animated big white blocks, but it doesn't matter how well something moves if you can't see what it's supposed to be. The graphics are those used in the Amstrad CPC and Commodore 64 versions, which were designed for a lower screen resolution in multiple colours. The Spectrum's monochrome rendering leaves them an incomprehensible mess.

So the game appears to be two

MacLeod's sword proves too heavy, allowing Fizir to stab him in the eye.

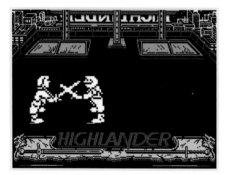

Due to illness, The Kurgen has been replaced by Toad of Toad Hall.

albino Lego models trying to smash each other apart with sticks. And as-

toundingly, it plays even worse than it looks. None of the sword fighting moves seem to do much – if you're lucky, then your opponent's energy may go down a bit, but you can't really tell who is successfully hitting whom. Generally a fight will last less than a minute as your opponent knocks you over in the corner and depletes your energy, at which point your head falls off. Your energy does start to regenerate if you don't attack or get hit for a second, but it's so hard to move away from your opponent that it's rarely useful.

The instruction manual tells you to watch for your enemy's attacks and respond to them, which is effectively impossible due to the clumsy movements and horribly unresponsive controls. You could only effectively respond to an opponent's attack if he sent you details on a postcard a week in advance. The single tactic that seems to have any effect at all is to mash the fire button and hope, turning *Highlander* into a slapstick routine of two nitwits flailing sticks at each other until one falls over.

The sound is almost non-existent. There is no music whatsoever and just a weird, popping noise if someone gets hit. And the laziness doesn't end there – despite there being three different opponents that you have to load separately, they all have identical moves. They just look different, and some can take more of a beating. I can only assume that *Highlander* must have been written in an incredible hurry.

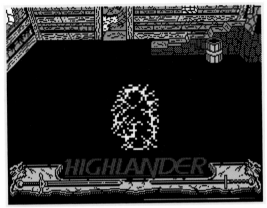

Ramírez absorbs the "quickening" energy from MacLeod's corpse, which seems to turn him into some kind of mole-man.

Have you ever tried to get an elderly relative to play a video game? *Highlander* is a way to experience the confusion and bewilderment they feel, even if you're well versed with the medium yourself. What's going on? Why isn't the little man moving? Why does he keep falling over? Why can't I ever win? Can I stop playing and watch *Columbo* now?

Playing *Highlander* is one of the least entertaining ways you could possibly spend your time. The fighting feels futile, as if you're just wasting your time watching some unnecessarily large white pixels move around. At least there's a simultaneous two player option so you can have a companion in your misery – until they leave and never speak to you again because you made them play *Highlander*.

Developers Canvas also made the crappy TV tie-in *Miami Vice*. But they also produced conversions of the excellent golf game *Leaderboard* and the graphic adventure *Killed Until*

The Amstrad CPC version kindly displays what the characters should actually look like.

Dead, which may have the greatest name of any game ever.

Ocean Software were an absolute powerhouse in the 8-bit days, releasing a huge number of licensed games as well as original titles. The peak of their success on the Spectrum was the brilliant *Robocop*, which broke records for the longest time spent at number one in the Gallup sales chart. They eventually became the UK arm of Infogrames and released their last game in 1998.

This wasn't the last attempt at a game based around *Highlander*. Nine years later, Lore Design Ltd made *Highlander: The Last of the MacLeods* for the Atari Jaguar, based

REVIEW SCORES

Sinclair User absolutely slammed the game, describing it as a "Golden Turkey" and awarding it 2/5. *Crash* described it as "totally boring and quite unplayable" yet gave it a stupidly inflated 57%. Oddly the other major Spectrum magazine *Your Sinclair* didn't review the game, but it did deservedly appear in their reader poll of worst games ever.

OTHER VERSIONS

Amstrad CPC: This version is far prettier and is the definitive Highlander experience for what that's worth. It received around 50% in reviews.
Commodore 64: This is also much better but runs slower than the other versions. It was absolutely reviled by reviewers – ZZap!64 magazine gave it 30% and revised the rating to 19% when it was re-released five years later at a cheaper price.

on a spin-off cartoon series. It was an interesting game ruined by an overly simple plot and abysmal controls, but it was still far better than *Highlander*. There was also an original game in production from Eidos Interactive for the Xbox 360, Playstation 3 and PC, but it was cancelled in 2010.

N THE EARLY NINETIES, software support for Atari's 8-bit line of computers began to dry up, leaving the format with a dwindling supply of new games. This led to mail order companies, like Germany's Power Per Post (PPP), becoming increasingly important to diehard enthusiasts. This is a shame, really, as it meant they were able to sell them unadulterated garbage like Hunter.

An attempt to recreate the sporting pastime of fatally wounding wild animals by shooting them with a big gun, Hunter spectacularly fails on several levels. It also spectacularly fails at being a video game that anyone could enjoy playing, so at least it's consistent.

The title screen is promising – a majestic, golden stag stands in front of a stylised sunrise as a funky, crunchy, bass-heavy chiptune plays. Oddly, the music doesn't fit the displayed image or the feel of hunting in a forest at all, implying that it was produced for something else entirely. It is good quality, but sadly this is the last time anything from Hunter will feel as if any effort was put into it.

I am resorting to using a screenshot of the menu, as all of the in-game shots look the same.

After dismissing the title screen, four options present themselves, together with another totally incongruous tune. Or possibly three options, as it doesn't actually seem possible to change the "level" setting. It is, however, possible to select ammo values of 80, 160 and 240, the higher numbers doing nothing more than stretching the game out past the point of sanity. It's also possible to turn the sound off completely – and as the only sound is the same astonishingly ill-fitting music played constantly throughout the game, that may be a good idea.

On starting the game, you are treated to a single static scene of two trees on a grassy landscape. And that's it

I hope you like this scene, as you won't be seeing any others. Ever.

location-wise, as there is no movement or alternate scenery. The animals, for reasons best known to themselves, start sliding across the screen from right to left. And I mean they literally slide – there is no animation at all, meaning that the animals look like cardboard cut-outs drifting across the screen on roller skates. Once one has disappeared off to the left, another appears immediately and slides across in almost exactly the same place; there are only a few pixels of height variation between the paths they take. The beasts must have politely formed a queue to glide along a hidden train track and be shot one at a time. You can't really blame the hunter for not moving location after finding a hunting ground like that...

Your job, of course, is to stop the animals from reaching the left

From left to right we have: Slug / rabbit hybrid (2 points), Dog with head-mounted helicopter blades (4 points), Sock-faced elk (5 points).

side of the screen by killing them dead with bullets. This is achieved by moving a circle over the animal and pressing fire. In order to stop that being too easy, the crosshair circle jerks and flickers around to an insane extent. It's not just like the hunter has unsteady hands, it's like he's operating a pneumatic road drill at the same time as aiming. (But on the plus side, "Jerky Crosshair" is an amazing name for a tongue-in-cheek Country and Western music act.)

If you're lucky enough to press the fire button at the exact moment the circle flails over the animal, then the animal instantly evaporates – a major disappointment for any hunter wanting meat or a trophy, although you do get some points. This task is made easier by your gun being fully

automatic, holding all its ammunition in one clip and having a fire rate of approximately 480 rounds a minute. As all the animals take the same path, the most effective strategy is just to position the circle where you know all of them are going to pass and leave it there. You simply hold down the fire button as your prey reaches the circle and release it when they've vanished into the ether. Then the next creature from the queue immediately starts sliding across, and this continues until you run out of ammo. At no point do you enjoy yourself.

Hunter's only shred of variety is that there are three different mammals to slay, they appear in random order, and they are worth different points.

Yet another intrinsic flaw with *Hunter* is that the smaller animals that give

Here we see the crosshair circle in full jitter. Excitement fails to ensue.

fewer points are actually harder to shoot. As there is no time limit and an infinite supply of woodland creatures with a death wish, the best plan is to ignore the slugrabbits and only shoot at the helidogs and sockelks in order to conserve ammunition.

The game finally ends when your bullets run out. At this point, a text box appears telling you that when your ammo hit zero, you turned around and ran away, accidentally smacked into a deer and fell over, and had to spend a few days in hospital. A final insult, although it's at least more colourful than just saying Game Over.

Hunter ends up not being a hunting game at all; instead it seems to focus on a jittery-handed lunatic wielding a huge automatic rifle and raking in an endless stream of wheeled cardboard cut-outs at the edge of a forest. Somehow I doubt this is what the programmers set out to achieve.

This is one of the most egregious examples of a game being knocked out quickly for the cash that I've ever come across. The whole thing feels unfinished on a conceptual level, let alone a practical one. The only decent part is the music, which was clearly not written for the game and was presumably only used because Condor Soft had access to it. I'm filing this one under "Cheeky to charge money for it".

Some PPP games were translated into English and sold by companies in the UK and America, but for reasons that should by now be painfully obvious, they decided to give *Hunter* a miss. I was unable to find any published reviews of the game, but I really, really hope that a German magazine somewhere was able to warn its readers against throwing money at this quarter-arsed semi-game.

PPP continued to sell games with such evocative titles as *Rubber Ball* and *Glaggs It!* well into the 90s. Condor Soft made no other games at all – presumably as they'd already brought the world a premier cardboard-elk-on-roller-skates-shooting simulator, they had nothing else to strive for.

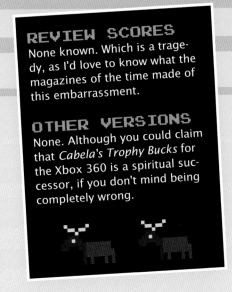

REVIEW SCORES

None known. Which is a tragedy, as I'd love to know what the magazines of the time made of this embarrassment.

OTHER VERSIONS

None. Although you could claim that *Cabela's Trophy Bucks* for the Xbox 360 is a spiritual successor, if you don't mind being completely wrong.

THE MOST DISAPPOINTING GAME I EVER BOUGHT

BY PAUL ROSE AKA MR BIFFO, EDITOR OF FORMER TELETEXT GAMES MAG, DIGITISER-TURNED-SCREENWRITER

JACK AND THE BEANSTALK
FORMAT: ZX SPECTRUM
YEAR OF RELEASE: 1984
DEVELOPER: CHRIS & STEVE KERRY
PUBLISHER: THOR COMPUTER SOFTWARE
ORIGINAL PRICE: 5.95 POUNDS

I WAS SUCKED IN by the graphics on the packaging of Jack and the Beanstalk – which, at least in screenshot form, did a fair job of aping the Ultimate Play the Game aesthetic. Not only did it not live up to the promised visuals, it was infuriatingly difficult. I don't think I ever got past the first level, which had Jack attempting to scale the beanstalk while being knocked off it by the endlessly-circling birds.

I was disappointed, naturally – but more than that, I felt cheated out of my pocket money. Consequently, I attempted to erase the tape using a magnet, then went to my parents and told them that there was something wrong with it. My dad took me back to the shop to get a refund, but the manager refused – of course, he tested out the game, and it worked fine. My dad pressed the point, getting increasingly angry, until the manager caved and said he'd replace it, but only with another copy of the same game. This led to a horrible escalation of events, which culminated in my dad using a racist term and storming out of the shop. The guilt of it haunts me to this day.

The horrible domino effect caused by my initial deceit utterly scarred me. I became much, much more cautious lest any knee-jerk purchases led to a further display of my dad's hitherto – and subsequent – buried racism.

Paul can be found at www.digitiser2000.com and on Twitter at @mrbiffo

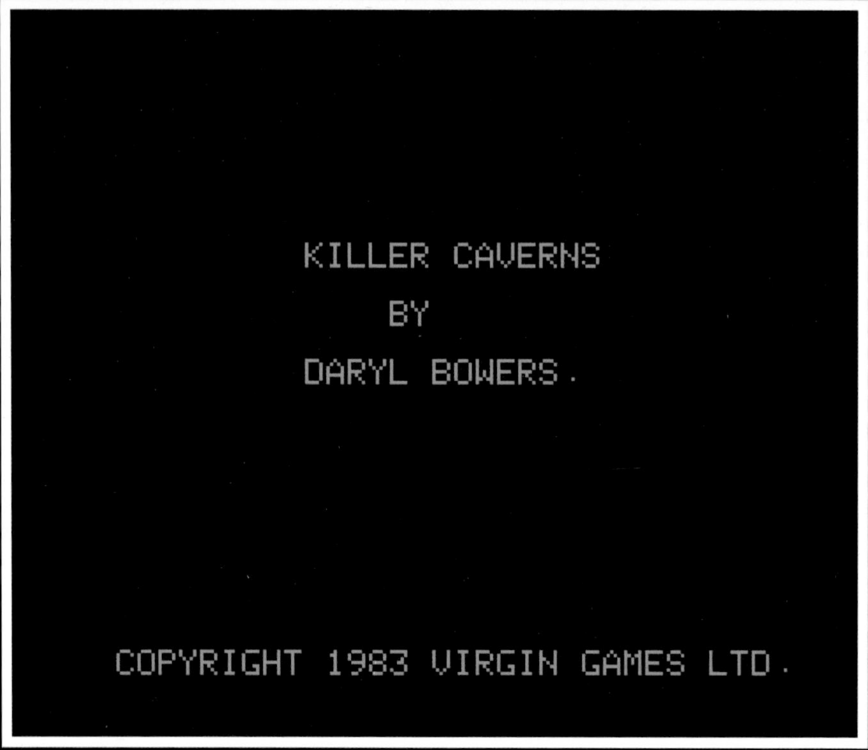

KILLER CAVERNS

BY

DARYL BOWERS.

COPYRIGHT 1983 VIRGIN GAMES LTD.

KILLER CAVERNS

FORMAT: ORIC-1
YEAR OF RELEASE: 1983
DEVELOPER: DARYL BOWERS
PUBLISHER: VIRGIN GAMES

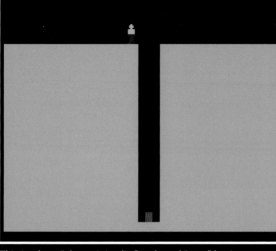

This is where "ultra-minimalist" ends and "crap" begins.

HAVE YOU BEEN waiting all your life for a game about caverns that kill people? Well even if so, I cannot recommend this game. Sorry.

Killer Caverns tells the story of Helpless Harold, a man desperate to get his hands on a certain treasure chest. Usefully, he starts the game standing near it! But less usefully it's at the bottom of a well, and he can't actually reach it. So rather than go and get a rope or something, he decides to search through a nearby cavern system full of lethal dangers to retrieve seventeen parts of a ladder that a madman hid there. Helpless Harold is not a clever man.

The game begins by asking you to select a difficulty from 1-9, but it doesn't seem to make any difference whatsoever when you play. In fact, nothing you do makes much difference, but we'll come to that later.

Killer Caverns is graphically primitive, even for the time. The treasure chest is literally a red block, the caverns have flat, purple ceilings containing pencils of varying length, and Harold himself looks like the logo for a courier service. There is very little sound, save for an occasional hiss made by one of the cavern's traps.

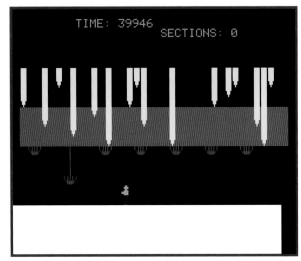

TIME: 39946
SECTIONS: 0

I think these are spiders. They could also conceivably be crabs or defective wigs.

There are only two controls: one for moving left and one for moving right. Harold seems incapable of jumping as well as basic human reasoning. From the starting location next to the treasure-bearing well, you move left and keep going in the hope of stumbling over a bit of ladder. There is no route selection, you just repeatedly go from right to left.

Some screens are empty, but most contain some kind of horrifying, deadly problem you need to get past. These are:

· Spiders on the roof that randomly lower themselves

· A deadly jet of steam that randomly appears

· A set of spikes that randomly fall from the ceiling

· A giant blue snake/worm thing that randomly pops up from the floor

· A flying scorpion that randomly floats around the screen making comical noises, as if it's propelled by flatulence

You will notice that each obstacle has the word "randomly" in its description, and therein lies the absolute downfall of the game. Every danger appears and disappears entirely at random,

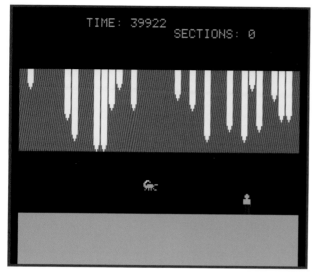

Farty the Floating Scorpion in action. Heaven help us.

meaning it's impossible to time your run past them. You may as well just hold left and hope, as trying to assert any control over your character is totally pointless. You've heard the phrase "more luck than judgement"? Well *Killer Caverns* is all luck and no judgement. It may as well be a coin-tossing simulator.

There's also precious little variety in the caverns you run through. I could only find the five obstacles listed above and the occasional piece of ladder inexplicably suspended from the ceiling. You frequently run through the same screen twice in a row, and sometimes three or more times. Occasionally you die immediately on entering a cavern, which could either be due to a bug or extreme bad luck with the random obstacles. Either way it's bad news, as you only have five lives, although depositing an umbrella piece down the well earns you an extra one.

On the plus side, as the game is written in BASIC, it's trivially easy to get more lives. You can just break into the program and change a single

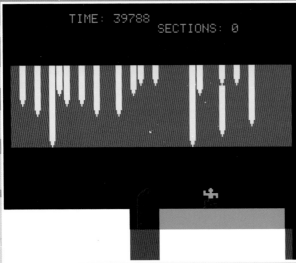

TIME: 39788   SECTIONS: 0

Kingseeker Frampt from Dark Souls makes his first video game appearance.

was full price at the time. It looks awful, plays badly, and ultimately there's no point in playing it at all. The final insult is that after the game ends, it asks if you want to play again with a Y/N prompt. Pressing N does nothing, and it simply waits forever for you to press Y. Curse you, *Killer Caverns*.

Virgin's game releases of the time featured a photo and a mini-interview with the programmer, from which we learn that *Killer Caverns* was written by a 15-year-old schoolboy called Daryl who played synthesiser in a local band. It's hard to stay angry at him for this game though, as he seems like such a nice guy. If you completed his later Commodore 64 game *Cheap Skate*, it gave you his home phone number and invited you for a drink if you were

variable to give yourself as many lives as you'd like. The downsides to being written in BASIC are that the game is sluggish, the controls are unresponsive, and the collision detection is vague at best. Not that the last point really matters due to the random nature of the game...

Even in 1983, *Killer Caverns* was totally unacceptable, especially for what

Here is every single one of Helpless Harold's animation frames. You're welcome.

ever in Kings Lynn. Plus he went on to program the excellent C64 version of comedy war game *North & South*, which obviously redeems him.

Virgin only released one other game for the Oric – a strange collection of mini-games called – *Them: A Paranoid Fantasy* that was actually pretty good.

REVIEW SCORES

Personal Computer Games magazine gave it 1/10, declaring that "This game is so bad in so many respects, it amazes me how Virgin could have released such rubbish!"

OTHER VERSIONS

None whatsoever. If you want the authentic *Killer Caverns* experience, you'll have to get yourself an Oric. (I suggest going for the upgraded Atmos version as it has a cool black and red keyboard.)

Killjoy — 1996 Dancing Yak Productions

High Score
=========

Stuart — 9408

————————————

Instructions:

1. Shoot things.
2. Do not miss.
3. You have 3 lives.
4. That's it.

Controls:

Use the mouse.

Left mouse button to begin
Press ESCAPE to quit & save Hiscore

KILLJOY

FORMAT: COMMODORE AMIGA 1200
YEAR OF RELEASE: UNRELEASED (FINISHED 1996)
DEVELOPER: STUART ASHEN
PUBLISHER: UNPUBLISHED
ORIGINAL PRICE: N/A □ FREEWARE

Suit-man is about to shoot. The background and blood spatter continue to look dreadful.

BACK IN 1995 I was tinkering with AMOS Professional, a BASIC programming language for the Commodore Amiga. The main program had been included on a magazine cover disk, and I'd managed to find a copy of the associated machine code compiler at a car boot sale. All I'd actually made were a couple of novelty programs to amuse my friend Raymond, but I'd sent them off to the public domain libraries of the time anyway. Bolstered by the success of seeing the names of my programs listed as two tiny lines of text in a magazine, I decided the time was right to make an actual game.

Unfortunately I was painfully aware that whatever I made would have to be extremely simple, as my programming skills were pathetic. I decided to opt for a target shooting game, since all it effectively entailed was having the player click on things with the mouse. Even I could handle that. Unfortunately I still had to deal with my lack of artistic skills when it came to the game's graphics.

Sega's 3D light gun game *Virtua Cop 2* was popular at the time, and it made me realise that the graphics could be heavily stylised rather than traditionally drawn. Obviously full 3D was way beyond my abilities, and realistically those of the machine I was writing for, if I wanted the game to run at a decent frame rate. But there were

Everyone you shoot is me. It's like Hunt the Ashens or something.

other options. I had recently bought a device called Videomaster AGA that allowed me to import footage from a VHS recorder. A plan formed – I would borrow my dad's creaky Ferguson video camera, film myself arsing around in front of it, transfer the footage to my Amiga, and then draw over every other frame. This rotoscoping technique was rarely used in games at the time, but it worked incredibly well, giving the game a unique look. Sadly, every other aspect of *Killjoy* was awful.

After the loading message, which I entered as "Loading, please dance" (I thought "Please wait" was boring) the game starts up by telling you how much RAM your computer has free. This is totally useless information from the player's point of view, and it doesn't even help me as the programmer because AMOS manages the memory itself. It may as well tell you the average annual rainfall in Helsinki.

The title screen tells you to shoot things without missing in order to accumulate score, whilst various characters from ZX Spectrum games scroll past. This wasn't really an aesthetic choice – I was just excited that I'd got a Spectrum emulator and ripped a load of graphics from it. A jolly little tune called "Cabbage" plays in the background and in no way matches the feel of the game. Like all other sounds in Killjoy, I took it from somewhere else

My centre part haircut was the height of mid-90s fashion. (No it wasn't.)

is of an unbelievably poorly drawn road and a building full of windows. (I recall that it was a test background that I never got round to changing.) Featureless but realistically animated characters appear at the windows and shoot into the screen after a few seconds, unless you shoot them first. Other enemies run along the road, but they don't actually shoot or pose any threat; they just serve as a distraction. Occasionally, in a nod to *Virtua Cop*, people appear very close to the screen and try to slash it with a knife or meat cleaver. Unfortunately the slashing effects are so badly drawn that it looks more like they've been drawn on the screen with a red crayon.

- in this case I'd found it on a public domain disk somewhere.

So before the game begins, we have irrelevant information, graphics and music. This total lack of cohesive design is a feature of most of my early projects, in which I was overexcited by disparate ideas and threw them all together to the detriment of the overall enterprise.

The game itself is barebones and frankly not much fun. The single view

And that's it really. You just have to shoot as many people as possible before you lose all three of your lives. It becomes easy after a bit of practice, but you'll still be killed off by an annoying bug that makes your shots go

Bang! One life gone. Green-man here is the only character not rotoscoped from my movements – the running animation is taken from Jodie Foster at the very beginning of Silence of the Lambs.

The Killjoy cast: Suit-man, Shirt-man, Green-man, Hazmat-man.

straight through the melee of attackers about a third of the time. Other exciting programming errors include duplicating corpses and the ability to kill the people who appear in the building by shooting the frame of the window they're in. Also, the game only works on higher specification A1200 computers when it could easily run on the standard A500 machines.

When you do finally succumb to the onslaught of rotoscoped maniacs, the game plays the clichéd soundbite of Hudson from Aliens shouting "Game over, man!" and you're presented with statistics showing how many shots you fired and what percentage of them hit their mark. That's actually one of the few features I'm pleased with, as it adds an extra element to the game – making you try to keep your accuracy at 100%. Or at least you might do if the game was enjoyable in any way.

Killjoy isn't actually as bad as I remembered. It's utter rubbish, of course, but it might actually be possible to enjoy yourself playing it for a minute or so before the bugs and boredom force you to play something else. The sprites still look well animated and are vaguely reminiscent of *The Last Express*, an excellent PC game released the following year that made heavy use of rotoscoping to much better effect. But everything else about *Killjoy* is concentrated arse wash.

At one stage, I had plans to make a bonus round where you had to shoot an apple off a person's head while hin-

All that remains of my next game – a hacking simulator – are these icons. Why are "Mail" and "Upload" written lower down than "Dial" and "Analysis"? RUBBISH.

dered by the targeting crosshair flickering around. I put together a test version, but it simply wasn't any fun so I abandoned it. Many years later, I discovered *Hunter* for the Atari 8-bit computers is exactly that idea but stretched to fill an entire game. It's amazing to think that only a year previously, people were charging money for something I considered too crap to include with a low-quality freeware title...

I finished *Killjoy* in early March 1996. Before I compiled it properly, a murderer shot dead sixteen primary school children and a teacher in the Scottish town of Dunblane. That made me decide the world didn't need a plotless game where you shoot random people, so *Killjoy* was never released.

Shortly after, I started to write another game – a kind of hacking

simulator set in the early eighties and based on the 8-bit games Hacker and SATCOM. I put together the game's back end but never actually added any content, as the Amiga was on its last legs. Instead I got a PC, and then an internet connection the next year, and I started writing comedy articles instead of substandard games.

REVIEW SCORES
No reviews – the game wasn't released, and freeware games were rarely reviewed at the time anyway.

OTHER VERSIONS
None.

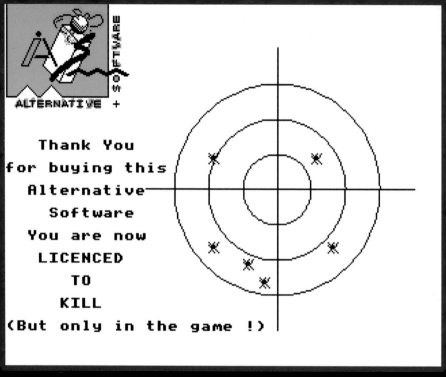

LICENCE TO KILL

FORMAT: ACORN ELECTRON
YEAR OF RELEASE: 1987
DEVELOPER: SIMON GUEST & J. HAMBLETT
PUBLISHER: ALTERNATIVE SOFTWARE
ORIGINAL PRICE: 1.99 POUNDS

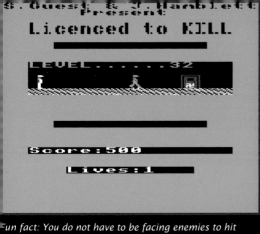

Fun fact: You do not have to be facing enemies to hit them. This is not a good game.

BEFORE I DELVE INTO the well of fetid bum rot that is *Licence to Kill*, I need to make it clear that it has nothing to do with the James Bond film of the same name. That was released two years later, and the tie-in game wasn't released for the Electron. Here ends the public service message.

Another entry on the list of old budget games that couldn't decide what they were called, the cover of this same proclaims the title to be *Licence*

to Kill, but the actual in-game text calls it *Licenced to Kill*. I'm going with the name on the case because it seems more official, and it's one less letter to type.

On loading, *Licence to Kill* presents you with 27 seconds of a black screen with occasional fart noises. The noises seem to be gunshot effects for the target logo that eventually appears and gets riddled with bullet holes. So far, so weird.

You are then given an amazingly long list of instructions for a budget game. The plot revolves around you being a top secret agent who must infiltrate a factory that has been taken over by a "neonasty organisation" to recover a valuable prototype. There are various digs at the ZX Spectrum in the names used – the factories are owned by "Sink-Lair" and the villains are known as the "Surclives", references to Sinclair Research and its founder Sir Clive. Even the prototype is called the "CZ 3/4" which pokes fun at Sinclair's

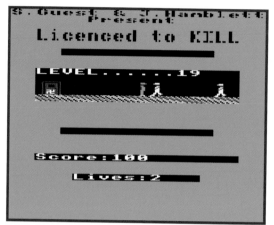

Our hero stands impassively, accepting that his imminent death is unavoidable.

ill-fated electric tricycle, the C5.

In order to retrieve the prototype, you need to get access codes from six different computers whilst collecting cassettes, keys and a disk. Enemy robots will hinder your mission by trying to murder you, but you're armed with an electromagnetic screwdriver which makes them teleport away when you prod them with it.

Got all that? Excellent! Now to start the game and wish you were doing almost anything else.

The title screen is a hideous slab of green with black bars and an ugly custom font plastered on it. The title music seems to consist mostly of randomised, discordant beeping. A thin strip near the top of the screen has some text scrolling in it. You start the game and discover that the thin strip is *the whole of the play area.*

It's like you lost the keys to your house and are having to play the game looking through the letterbox. Amazingly, *Licence to Kill* uses only 12.5% of the available screen area for gameplay. There isn't even a lot of status information shown on the rest of the screen – it's nearly all empty!

The graphics are about as basic as you can get. The almost featureless main character has two frames of walking animation and a frame for jabbing with his screwdriver... and that's the lot. The enemies are just palette swaps of the main character.

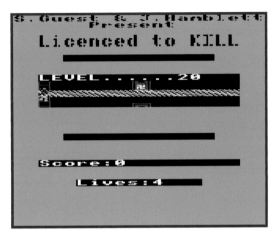

This is what happens when you climb the ladder. Not pictured: deep regret for playing this game at all.

Each floor appears identical. You move right and your character shuffles along at high speed, a shrieking bleep accompanying every single step he takes.

After a few seconds, the enemies appear and rush towards you from both in front and behind. You press the return key for a screwdriver jab, and chances are you instantly die. This is because the stabbing animation only appears for a tiny fraction of a second and doesn't seem to work all the time, and the enemies jolt along the screen so fast you can't time the attack properly. Actually hitting an enemy is largely down to blind luck – and when you do manage it, they sometimes just teleport right next to you anyway.

The floor looks like a rope made out of unravelled Christmas jumpers. And the only background features are red doors, each of which is marked with a swastika. So rather than the game being set in a robot-infested factory as the instructions state, it actually seems to be set in a Nazi base of some kind.

You start off on the 32nd level of the astonishingly tall "factory" next to a ladder, which you can use to climb down to any of the other 31 floors.

By employing super-human patience I was able to actually run a fair distance along several of the levels, but I encountered absolutely nothing except for background doors that are just for show. The levels seem to go on

```
          Classified Agents
1      J.R. WAS A        10000
2      BAD GUY,BUT        9000
3       I BET YOU         8000
4       CAN'T TOP         7000
5         HIM!            6000
6       IF YOU GET        5000
7       A HI-SCORE        4000
8        YOU WILL         3000
9       RUIN THIS         2000
10       MESSAGE!         1000
      Press space bar to continue.
```

This is the high score table with default entries! Because we've seen quite enough of the in-game graphics.

I actually hate *Licence to Kill*. I have pretty neutral feelings about most of the games in this book and mostly think of them as amusing curiosities. But there's something about the sheer disdain this game seems to have for the player – and by extension the buyer – that makes me want to punch it right in the tape spool. It's painfully difficult, as progression is based more on blind luck than skill. The insultingly small letterbox that the game plays in is utterly unnecessary. Most of the game's described features don't actually seem to exist – or might as well not exist. The stated plot seems to have no bearing on the game, which actually seems to be about infiltrating a Nazi base armed with a knife. The high score table plays an off-key version of the cancan. And worst of all, it's called *Licence to Kill* but features no killing, just forcibly teleporting

forever, and at no stage did I see anything to pick up or any computers to interact with for codes. I had a look online, and nobody else who played the game seems to have either. Are the instructions mentioning non-existent features and the game is actually a sham, with nothing to actually do? Or is it just so insanely difficult that nobody has ever got far enough to find anything?

Every frame of animation for the main character. I reckon that's a knife and not an "electromagnetic screwdriver".

androids. This game hates me and I hate it right back.

It's amazing that a game this primitive and dreadful was released so late in the Electron's life. If the cassette inlay didn't clearly state the copyright date as 1987, I'd have thought it was a bad mail-order title from 1983.

Alternative Software released a slew of budget games across most of the 8-bit computer formats. Many of them were poor, to the extent that two of them are featured in this book. The development dream team of Guest & Hamblett also made incompetent *Breakout* clone *Spheroids* (AKA *Round Ones*) and the horrifying, flickery mess *Indoor Soccer*, making them the equivalent of war criminals in the Electron world.

REVIEW SCORES
No known reviews. I imagine the staff of *Electron User* magazine hid in the basement for a week when they heard it was being released. A wise choice.

OTHER VERSIONS
None. I am pleased to report that all other platforms remained free of *Licence to Kill*.

THE STATE OF THE INDUSTRY

STE PICKFORD is a veteran games designer, graphic artist, and half of the Pickford Bros with his brother John. The Pickfords have worked on over 36 games since 1984 and were responsible for many successful, critically acclaimed budget games including *180*, *Feud*, and *Zub* and *Amaurote*, as well as full price releases such as *Glider Rider* and *Plok!* Here's some insight into the industry that spawned the terrible games in this book, from someone who made good ones...

MY INSIGHT INTO the industry comes largely from my time working at Binary Design Limited which was a fairly large place (at least by the standards of the time).

It was actually a pretty professionally run place in many ways, probably ahead of its time as a proper, work-for-hire development studio in the mid-80s, which I don't think was especially common. There were maybe a couple of other places around the country similar to Binary Design, making games for budget developers like Mastertronic, but I think bedroom coders – amateur

teams, essentially – made a good chunk of budget games. It was a weird mix. About half of budget games were made by teenagers in their bedrooms, and the other half were made at reasonably professional, large studios with several teams and multiple projects on the go at any one time.

I'm not sure you'd be able to tell by playing the games which were made by professional studios and which were made by amateurs at home. We weren't necessarily making better games, but we were probably making them more quickly. I guess

Beautiful loading screen for Feud on the Amstrad CPC.

the budget publishers weren't getting enough games sent in on spec, so they had to commission more to satisfy the market.

Interestingly, at Binary Design we also developed full price games for Quicksilva and some other publishers. There was absolutely no difference in how we developed full price or budget games. I don't know if the money was any better (the boss never shared that information), but in terms of deadlines, which team was given the gig, how much effort we put in, etc., full price and budget games got exactly the same treatment.

The full price publishers generally had a clearer idea of what type of genre they wanted (a flight simulator, future sport, etc.), whereas Mastertronic were more hands-off and just wanted it on time, but neither were very strong on judging quality or playability. That was really down to us. All that publishers were really bothered about was if a game was late or if there were serious bugs.

We (the development team) were really the only ones who cared about the quality of the games. The reason we were always late was because we were determined to make our games good, if we could. We took some pride in our work, we wanted players to like the games and we wanted good reviews. I don't recall any publisher caring about how a game would review while it was in development, although they were pleased

The brilliant darts game 180 for the Spectrum. I played it so much that I became dart-perfect.

with good reviews after release.

Binary Design definitely wasn't a tiny operation. They were about as big as development studios got in those days, and may well have been the biggest in the UK at the time. They just developed a lot of games for budget publishers.

When I started at Binary Design, the setup was five "teams", each of which consisted of an island of three desks pushed together in a large, open plan office. One of each team's desks was home to the ZX Spectrum programmer, one to the C64 pro-grammer, and one to the Amstrad CPC programmer. All three members of the team would be writing the same game, each for their respective platforms (other conversions, like MSX or Atari were handled by free-lancers). One of the three would be the designated lead programmer, which usually meant they designed the game as well. Depending on the game and the relative skill of the programmers, the lead would either write the game and the other two programmers convert the code, or they'd each write essentially separate versions of the same game better suited to their platform. Sometimes the ZX Spectrum and Amstrad programmers would write the game together, sharing code (each guy writing different Z80 "subroutines" shared between both versions), and the C64 programmer would write something different (6502 code, using C64 specific hardware sprites and scrolling, which couldn't be shared).

Music and sound were handled by a separate department comprising one musician (David Whittaker when I started – my line manager), and two

Strategy and action collide in Death Wake, much like the aircraft and bullets seen here.

or three graphic artists. We would provide sprites and backgrounds and loading screens for each of the five projects and their three versions, on an ad hoc basis. Mainly it was who asked first, or who seemed most in need. At one point our boss tried to introduce a "graphic request form" system, in which programmers had to submit forms listing a sprite or tile or something they needed, and we had to draw whatever was on the form at the top of the list, but that didn't work very well. It was easier to talk to the teams and judge for ourselves what was needed and in what order.

Deadlines were always an issue, though – we never felt we had long enough. My brother's very first project (*Death Wake* for Quicksilva) was given eight weeks. He was a new employee and didn't even know machine code at the time, so he was learning assembler while developing the game. He took 12 weeks and was in some trouble for being so late. Generally I think we had around 16 weeks for most games (and it was the same for budget or full price), but we always took a few weeks longer and were always slightly in trouble for being late.

We would be scheduled to have, say, half a day allocated to getting the main character moving (this was in *Zub* on the Spectrum that John was programming). John spent half a day getting it working, but it didn't feel quite right. It wasn't enjoyable to simply run and jump. So John spent the rest of the day tweaking the feel of the jump and the movement. He might alter the speed of animation, or I might tweak the pixels in a frame of animation or add a new frame; then John would alter the strength of

In school I became so enamoured of the Zub character that I drew comic strips about him for my friend Phil. I hope he doesn't still have them.

movement. This pattern repeated itself over the development of the whole game (and every other game we worked on) – the boss's main focus was finishing on time, and our main focus was making the game good.

When the game was finished, two weeks late, we were in trouble for "costing the company money", but very often our games went on to sell really well, bring in royalties, and (I'm certain) help the company secure future work. The games made by some of the other teams that were on time were often the most forgettable games that nobody cared about and didn't sell. So we used to argue that we were actually the ones making the company money. There

gravity and maybe the speed of movement, or add an extra delay before taking off from a crouch, etc. John would play it and tweak it until he was happy. All told I think the running and jumping in *Zub* took two days. John was then in trouble for making the game one and a half days late as only half a day had been allocated to main character

Plok! The Exploding Man for the Super Nintendo. Ste currently draws a comic about the character.

The Pickfords also made Wizards & Warriors 3 *for the NES. I'm only mentioning this so I can show this amusing sprite.*

was always tension between us and the boss, though, about being good or being on time.

As the 80s progressed, the industry began to change. The biggest shift was the switch to 16-bit. That was a massive transition, essentially increasing the number of artists needed on a team. With the 8-bit games, we had about three artists servicing 15 programmers (ok, that was five projects with three versions each, so some of the graphics were shared between games). With the 16-bit stuff, however, it got closer to one artist per programmer on each project, and more in some cases.

Toward the very end of the 80s, the consoles started to appear. We got in with Nintendo stuff earlier than most, so we switched from 16-bit to NES development around '88, whereas it was probably early 90s for most other British studios.

The switch to console was MASSIVE. Basically, we had to make games that were genuinely good – that £40 price tag meant the game had to offer a lot more value than a £1.99 game – and we had to make games that were bug-free. We scoffed at first – it was impossible to make bug-free games – but that was the requirement, and we did it, by and large. Console development was a big, big step up in professionalism.

WHICH OF YOUR BUDGET GAMES ARE YOU MOST PROUD OF?

I'd say *Feud*. That was the first project where John designed the game but wasn't the programmer. We actually sold the design to the company, with the map I drew being part of the game design, rather than something created during development. So this was our first experience of being game designers rather than game developers, and of designing a game before development started. The project was a success as well (on Spectrum and Amstrad at least), and it was a game where the actual design of it mattered and worked. As well as doing the 8-bit graphics, I also got to do the Amiga graphics, which was my first taste of 16-bit graphics work. I have extra fond memories of it for that reason.

In Feud, two brothers attempt to murder each other with magic. The Pickford Bros assure me it is not autobiographical.

WHAT WAS THE MOST DISAPPOINTING GAME YOU EVER PAID MONEY FOR?

Probably something big. There were loads of games that promised epic experiences but failed to deliver. Maybe *Valhalla*? I was expecting some epic adventure, and all I got was a buggy mess.

Ste is still making video games and drawing comic strips. He can be found at www.zee-3.com/pickford-bros/ and on Twitter at @stepickford

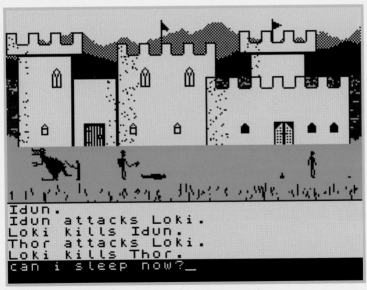

```
Idun.
Idun attacks Loki.
Loki kills Idun.
Thor attacks Loki.
Loki kills Thor.
can i sleep now?_
```

Valhalla spoils the ultimate ending to the Avengers movies.

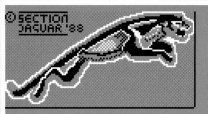

L.A.SWAT

GUEST ENTRY
from "Guru" Larry Bundy Jr, a British gaming television presenter who likes nothing more than to talk about obscure old video games in a humorous manner.

LOS ANGELES SWAT

FORMAT: AMSTRAD CPC
YEAR OF RELEASE: 1987
DEVELOPER: BEECHNUT CREATIVE SOFTWARE
PUBLISHER: ENTERTAINMENT USA (MASTERTRONIC)
ORIGINAL PRICE: 1.99 POUNDS

ONE OF THE WEEKLY HIGHLIGHTS for me as a child of the 80s was going with my parents to the newly built Tesco hypermarket in Watford for our big weekly shop. It was a huge, awe-inspiring building which (back then) was made to look like a converted village-barn-come-town-hall, complete with fake clock tower.

Halfway through our serial zigzagging of the many consumable-laden corridors, we came across an aisle presenting a vast collection of budget games for home computers. There were countless boxed cassettes, each pegged onto the wall in their own individual blister packs, and each one covered in exciting hand-drawn artwork, designed to separate young Johnny from his hard-earned pocket money.

Upon one of these many visits, one game's artwork in particular caught my eye – that of a tough-looking riot cop, all in black, with mirrored shades and baseball cap, and sporting a rather fetching Burt Reynolds-esque moustache. Police cars and vans sped in front of him as he brandished an assault rifle so bloomin' huge he could take out a tank with it. So to my

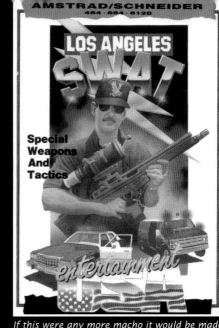

If this were any more macho it would be made of raw beef.

easily impressionable seven-year-old brain, it looked like the ultimate in awesomeness. Only a ninja dual wielding UZIs attached to nunchucks could possibly top it!

That game was *Los Angeles SWAT*

124

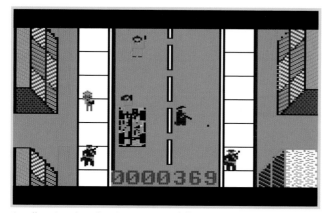

An all-action shot showing a granny falling apart and a SWAT team member shooting at a colleague.

hordes of baseball bat-wielding gang members and roof-based snipers, all whilst avoiding innocent grannies and burnt-out vehicles in the riot-stricken streets of L.A.

Maybe it was a political statement on the militarization of police forces in the USA, or maybe it was just an excuse to make the game not look like a complete rip-off of *Commando*. It was a reasonably entertaining arcade style shooter and played essentially the same across all formats... Well, all except the Amstrad CPC version. Guess which computer I had as a child?

To call the Amstrad version "crap" is an insult to excrement. After ten minutes of loading, you're treated to one of the laziest title images in history – a mostly blank screen with nothing on it aside from a poorly cropped image of

So I kissed goodbye my £1.99 and anticipated the excitement in my imminent future during my ride home from the supermarket.

Now, *Los Angeles SWAT*, or *L.A. SWAT* as everyone called it (the 80s loved its acronyms), is essentially a knock-off of Konami's arcade game *Jail Break*. You play a tough-as-nails riot cop, accompanied by two other officers (acting as your second and third lives) in a top-down, vertically scrolling shoot 'em up. You take on

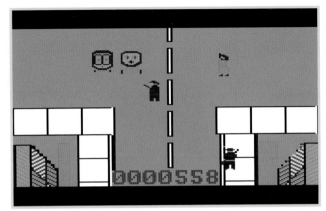

Head inflation is a rare side effect of a gunshot wound, yet it happens all the time in L.A. SWAT!

an extremely intimidating stick of liquorice.

Now Mr Stern is a feisty fellow. He will not only have seven or eight clones of himself on screen at the same time, but another will immediately take the place of one you killed the femtosecond he disappears, ultimately making killing them completely pointless – especially considering the main way to gain points in *L.A. SWAT* is to simply hold up on the joystick.

the Jaguar car company logo in the top left corner and the words "L.A. SWAT" in blocky italics. And things go downhill from there.

For starters, the programmer decided that he couldn't be bothered to program in the snipers or *any audio whatsoever*. There is only one enemy type in the game, and he resembles a Lego version of Daniel Stern's burglar character from *Home Alone*. He constantly spawns multiple clones of himself while viciously wielding

Luckily, the hordes of Daniels are easy to kill, as a single bullet from your rifle will cause his body to literally explode through his own eyeballs (yes, seriously). But, if he manages to break through your awkward, 30 degree angled firing lines, he will brutally murder you... and I mean *brutally*. Seriously, your corpse is just a pile of

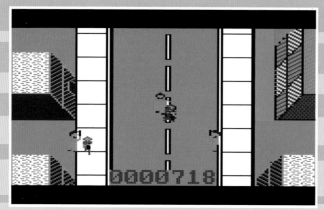

Our hero is smashed into a bloody pulp as two clones salute each other.

snipers, but gave up halfway through. Their bullets do actually appear randomly on-screen, floating in the middle of the street, but they can't hurt you and the animation has them travelling away from you...

To top it all off, it takes less than a minute to beat the entire game as the single street you traverse just repeats forever. It may sometimes last longer, but that's solely due to the enemies getting themselves stuck in upturned cars and you taking an extra few precious seconds to run around and find the optimal angle to kill them.

So why was the Amstrad port of *L.A. SWAT* so bad? Well, it all seems to come down to Mastertronic wanting to port the game to all systems. American developer Sculptured Software, the original creators of the game, worked on the majority of the ports. But as the

blood, bone and goo after he's finished with you!

But to be honest, the only legitimate danger is from the random grenades that the multiple clones occasionally throw in your direction. If they hit you, then confusingly they turn *you* into a dying Daniel Stern due to the game loading up the wrong death animation.

Speaking of which, the game is full of graphical glitches. For instance, it appears that the programmer at some point *tried* to code in the enemy

This is what happens when you complete level one. It's not a great incentive.

magazine's review of the game, which said, *"UCHI MATA is a pathetic piece of programming on what could have been a decent game."*

Larry can be found at youtube.com/larry and on Twitter at @LarryBundyJr

ZX Spectrum and the Amstrad CPC were British computers, those conversions was contracted out to an obscure and inexperienced local developer by the name of Beechnut Creative Software.

Beechnut must have been an extremely small company, as according to Google Maps, their place of operations was a terraced house on a council estate in Suffolk. Not only did Mastertronic never hire them again, but the only other Amstrad title they ever worked on was the judo simulator *Uchi Mata*. That scored 61% in Amtix

REVIEW SCORES

None known. It's almost as if Mastertronic didn't send any copies out for review!

OTHER VERSIONS

The Commodore 64 and Atari 8-bit versions are simple, slightly crude budget games that you could have some fun playing on a rainy afternoon. A very short rainy afternoon. The Spectrum version is a hideously ugly, jerky mess, but still far better than the diabolical Amstrad release.

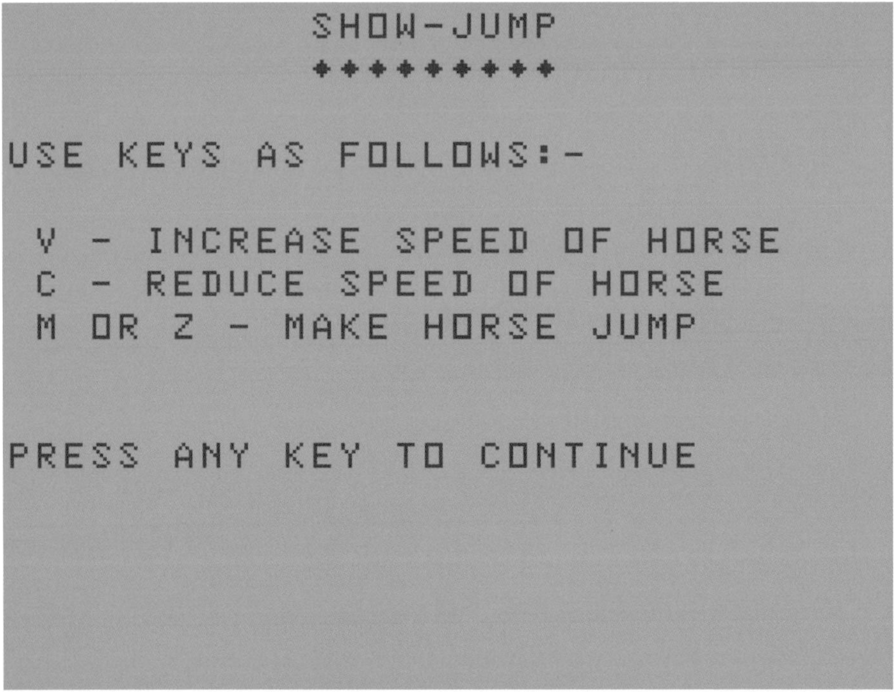

```
                SHOW-JUMP
                * * * * * * * * *


USE KEYS AS FOLLOWS:-

   V - INCREASE SPEED OF HORSE
   C - REDUCE SPEED OF HORSE
   M OR Z - MAKE HORSE JUMP



PRESS ANY KEY TO CONTINUE
```

SHOW-JUMP

FORMAT: DRAGON 32
YEAR OF RELEASE: 1985
DEVELOPER: UNKNOWN
PUBLISHER: COMPUTERWARE
ORIGINAL PRICE: 6.50 POUNDS

This is the puissance course, which means there is a big wall at the end. Or several, in this game.

IF YOU WERE making a video game about showjumping, to the extent of naming it after the activity, you'd at least look up how it was spelled, wouldn't you? Maybe the author had a load of spare hyphens lying around that needed to get used up.

Sadly this lack of basic effort leaks through into the whole game. Such were the joys of the mail-order industry for the more obscure computer formats in the 80s – you could release any old tat as long as the description was tempting.

Show-Jump is a painfully basic attempt to simulate a complicated equestrian event. The screen is split into eight horizontal strips, with the very top showing the number of faults and the rest showing a side view of the course. Your rider starts at the top left and when he reaches the right-hand side of the screen, he teleports to the left hand side of the next strip down which I believe rarely happens at actual show jumping events. Perhaps each segment represents the view from a different, super-ultra-widescreen television camera positioned equally along the course?

Your horse and rider are represented by a handful of dark blue pixels that look more like a St Bernard dog with a desk tidy on its back. There are only two frames of animation, and

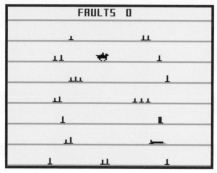

Tragedy strikes at the equestrian meet as a horse devolves into some kind of crab monster between jumps.

jumping involves the horse taking a short flight, complete with gradual take-off and landing. Fences are red sticks, and water hazards resemble unmade beds with garish duvet covers. Sound is limited to an ear-splitting bell at the start of a race, popping noises for the horse's hoof steps and some beeps if you hit an obstacle.

Gameplay is extremely simple. First you select one of the game's nine courses. Then you can control the horse's speed and make it jump, and that's your lot. The faster the horse goes, the further it leaps, so you need to slow down if there isn't much space between obstacles or you will land on them. But it's harder to time jumps the slower you're travelling, so the game is mostly about managing speed.

And here the game breaks its leg and has to be taken out of the paddock and shot. You can't actually tell how fast the horse is travelling as it has no discernible effect until you jump. The accelerate and decelerate controls don't seem to work effectively either, so you have no fine control over something you desperately need them for. It's frustrating as the jump control is extremely responsive and the collision detection seems spot on. I'm not saying that *Show-Jump* would be a good game if you could gauge speed, but it would at least be playable for a minute or two.

The simplicity of the gameplay is vaguely reminiscent of the "endless runner" genre of mobile games such as *Canabalt*, but lacking the finesse and compulsion that made those open-ended games so successful. (And it's also almost impossible to play effectively. Let's not forget that.)

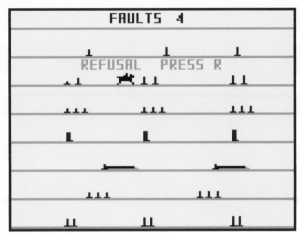

Fail to jump a hurdle and, understandably, your horse refuses to run headfirst into it.

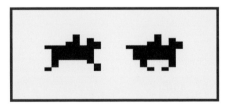

All the frames of animation used in Show-Jump. I believe there was no motion capture involved.

There is one commendable feature in the game: when you clip an obstacle, it gets the top taken off at the height you hit it. A single nice touch in a field of garbage.

No developer is credited for *Show-Jump*, so I can only assume that it was made in-house at Computerware by ninjas and ghosts. They only released a few games for the Dragon 32, mostly based on existing games like Scrabble and Blockbusters, and they're all much better than *Show-Jump*.

REVIEW SCORES
Dragon User magazine gave it 1/5 and described it as "boring" – a damning insult for any game.

OTHER VERSIONS
None. Phew.

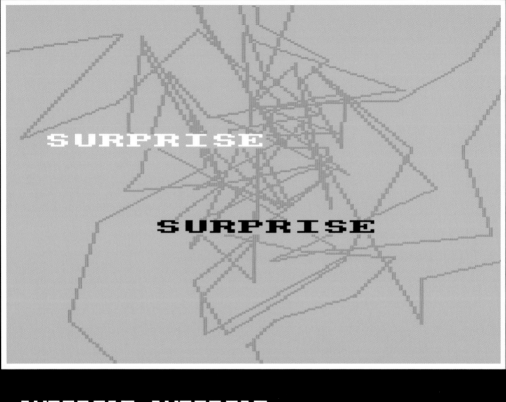

SURPRISE SURPRISE

FORMAT: AMSTRAD CPC (464 ONLY)
YEAR OF RELEASE: 1986
DEVELOPER: UNKNOWN
PUBLISHER: CENTRAL SOLUTIONS LTD
ORIGINAL PRICE: 1.99 POUNDS

Y IS MIDNIGHT. A hill over-
looks the city. A dark figure
stands atop it, gazing down
at the lights below. A cold
wind whips at its cloak but
t does not seem to feel it. A
small misshapen creature
scrabbles to the hilltop,
fear etched into its distort-
ed features. The dark figure
does not look away from
the city as it begins to
speak in a low, rasping
voice devoid of any positive
emotion.

This is from the game's intro sequence. Apparently that's a mansion.

"The plans have finally reached frui-
tion. Soon these people will know true
suffering."

The figure falls silent. Terrified, the
creature next to him speaks hesitant-
ly. "Master... Is it time?"

The dark figure turns towards the
creature. Under its cowl, its face is a
paper-white mask of evil – so twisted
by years of seething hatred that it is
barely recognisable as human. Its
mouth contorts into a terrifying mirth-
less grin as it spits out the words,
"Yes. Release *Surprise Surprise* for the
Amstrad CPC."

Surprise Surprise is a rare thing – a
game that seems to have been actively
designed to frustrate and annoy the
player to the point of illness. On loading you're presented with a head-
ache-inducing mess of flashing colours, random beeps and randomly
generated lines. The result is that your
screen looks like it has been smashed,
something you'll have the urge to do
in real life if you continue and actually
play the game.

The cassette inlay reveals a simple
plot. You've been invited to a banquet
in a 100-room mansion, but on entering you have to find four "clues" to

This is every single frame of animation for the main character.

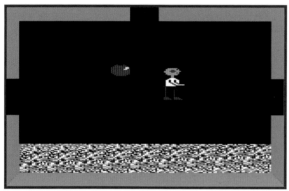

A red blob falls into some random pixels. Or possibly an apple falls onto the rainbow road to Asgard. Who can tell?

know what's on offer at the banquet, but it must be better than Turkey Twizzlers.

Surprise Surprise is absolutely hideous from the second you take control. The first thing you notice is the main character's ludicrous walking animations – moving left and right resembles a bizarre shuffle, and vertical movement involves his whole body staying rigid while his feet repeatedly dislocate themselves. In a strange design choice, his hair is only visible when he walks upwards.

Then you try playing the game, and any remaining hope you may have had for a fun experience evaporates into a cloud of pure hatred. Your character has a seemingly random walk speed: it starts off insanely sluggish in the first room and is even slower in others, to

reveal the banqueting hall. Also the mansion is full of lethal, giant fruit that flies around everywhere. Yet rather than realise your host is a complete maniac and leave immediately, you decide to take up the challenge! I don't

I apparently found a clue in this dead end! It took 34 seconds to walk to the bottom and then back up again. I hate this game.

the extent that some screens can take an entire minute to cross. In order to travel from one room to another you have to align yourself precisely with the door gaps or nothing happens, and the alignment isn't precisely based on what's visible which adds an extra layer of annoyance.

Add these points to dodgy collision detection and it can be almost impossible to avoid the enemies that float around the mansion. That is a shame, as if you touch any of them at any point, it is INSTANTLY game over. There are no lives and no continues. This game can incite levels of

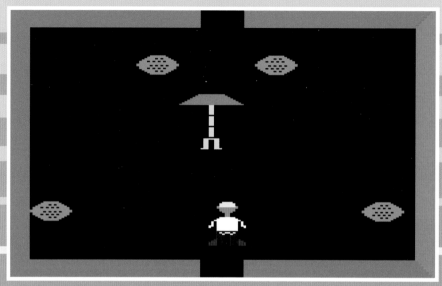

Our hero impersonates Eminem whilst being hassled by some giant floating limes near the very worst lamp Ikea sells.

frustration so extreme that they can cause nosebleeds.

But it's the sound that really pushes *Surprise Surprise* beyond the realms of normal annoyance to somewhere the mind of man should never go. Constantly playing in the background is a hideous cacophony of random bleepy percussion noises. It's like something designed to break the will of captured soldiers that was banned under the third Geneva Convention. And as you've probably guessed, there is no option to turn it off.

As for actually progressing through the game, I only found one of the elusive "clues." Upon walking to the bottom of a weird, brown corridor, the screen flashed and the inevitable Game Over screen appeared. I had apparently been awarded one point out of an available five. Any attempts to take another route through the house led to instant death at the hands of the almost unavoidable enemies. I am a patient man, but this game is actually painful to play.

The cover art is interesting because it shows a suit of armour shooting lightning from its hand, which has nothing to do with the game whatsoever. This attempt to hide the true nature of the game could possibly explain why it's called *Surprise Surprise*, as buyers were doubtless surprised by the hideous truth of their purchase. Or maybe the name was supposed to cash in on the television series *Surprise Surprise!* which was popular at the time.

When a game requires more patience than skill to progress, then its fundamental design is flawed. *Surprise Surprise* goes way beyond this to a point where it almost seems actively designed to cause the player discomfort. It is a grotesque mockery of an entertainment product.

The writer of the game remained anonymous, presumably so he or she could more easily escape with the money whilst laughing hysterically. Central Solutions Ltd only released two other Amstrad games – a terrible shoot 'em up called *Barchou* and the dull text adventure *Mansion*. They released a slew of other text adventures for the Spectrum, some well-regarded, but they never made the jump to the Amstrad.

REVIEW SCORES

Amstrad Action magazine awarded *Surprise Surprise* 10% and recommended that the reader buy a top of the line Amstrad CPC6128, simply because the game doesn't work on that model. And whilst I don't usually mention internet reviews, I'm going to give the last word to "Ritchardo" from his cpczone.emuunlim.org piece that gives the game zero out of ten: "I'm almost tempted to give it marks for the sheer bloody cheek of releasing this in the first place."

OTHER VERSIONS

None. Thank heaven for small mercies.

THE MOST DISAPPOINTING GAME I EVER BOUGHT

BY STEVE BENWAY, A RETRO GAMING COLLECTOR WHO PLAYS GAMES BADLY SO YOU CAN SEE WHAT THEY LOOK LIKE

URANIANS

FORMAT: ACORN ELECTRON
YEAR OF RELEASE: 1986
DEVELOPER: S. HOWITT
PUBLISHER: BUG-BYTE
ORIGINAL PRICE: 2.99 POUNDS

I WAS, AND STILL AM, a fan of single screen vertical shooters, so when I saw the screen shots on the back of the Uranians *cassette case, with lots of descending aliens, a mother ship at the top, and what looked like a really nice glowing effect, I was excited. Something like* Phoenix*, I thought. Pushing the system to the limit of its capabilities, I thought. Er... not quite.*

After the typical five minutes of loading from tape, I hit "play", and the very first thing that happened was the big mother ship dropped a super-fast bomb which landed a quarter of the way across the screen from me. "Hah! Missed!" would be a reasonable reaction to such a lame attack, except the bomb created an explosion that filled a third of the bottom of the screen. Half a second of gameplay... I hadn't even fired, and I'd already lost my first life.

It wasn't all bad. The movement of my ship was fast and responsive, though I'm guessing they used all the CPU cycles to do that, as the aliens' movement was predictable but jerky in a way that made them hard to shoot.

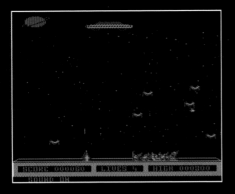

So that early death was just a bad start, you might wonder? Nope. The mother ship proceeded to dump those super-fast bombs with super-wide explosions on a regular basis, and even if they didn't kill you, the explosion would stay in place for around five to ten seconds, leaving you no room to move and allowing the aliens to pick you off.

That just leaves the impressive glowing effect of the graphics, shown in the screen grabs on the sleeve. Yeah, right. They'd just taken a photo of a TV screen, and the glow was from the screen.

Uranians? From Uranus? Yeah... I would say so.

I felt cheated and pretty bloody furious about it. The game was only £2.99, but as a young pup just out of school and suffering the exploitation of what was laughably called the Youth Training Scheme, I couldn't afford to just throw money away. However five minutes playing Uranians did make me want to throw my computer out of the window.

It didn't really change my attitude to buying games, though. I learned not to trust what was written or pictured on the case, but the problem was the Electron wasn't as common as the Spectrum or Commodore 64. As a result, the games were harder to find, and sometimes you just had to take what you could get. The sad truth is I was prepared to settle for really crappy games over no games at all.

Steve can be found on YouTube at https://www.youtube.com/user/SteveBenway and on Twitter at @SteveBenway

FACT! There's also a BBC Micro version which has much nicer music, but it is so fast it's almost uncontrollable.

SQIJ!

FORMAT: ZX SPECTRUM
YEAR OF RELEASE: 1987
DEVELOPER: JASON CREIGHTON
PUBLISHER: THE POWER HOUSE
ORIGINAL PRICE: 1.99 POUNDS

This was all there was to SQIJ! For any buyers who didn't understand the game's code well enough to fix the caps lock problem. Which was about 99% of them.

THIS IS IT. This is the worst game in this book. If anyone ever tells you that the worst commercially released game ever is *E.T.* for the Atari 2600 or *Big Rigs: Over the Road Racing* for PC, show them this. In fact, I'm not even sure this is technically a game. It was sold as a game, certainly, but it doesn't actually work as one.

SQIJ! is a conversion of a Commodore 64 game in which a mutant bird called "Sqij" lives in a post-apocalyptic world where food is running out. He must search some caves to find the parts of the Enertree which will provide an infinite supply of future comestibles. However the Spectrum version seems to focus on an immobile piece of folded paper sitting on the floor.

After starting *SQIJ* you are presented with what appears to be a huge origami bird stuck between two scribbles in a dark cave. The scribbles, which look like they've been drawn by a three-year-old girl with her mind on something else, slowly flicker up and down. Your score increases. And that's it forever.

None of the controls listed in the instructions work. No buttons do anything. That's what your £1.99 got you in 1987 – a piece of paper wedged between some flickering infant's

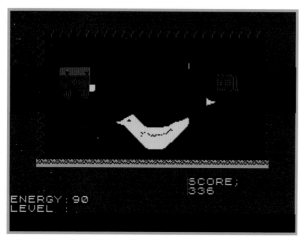

After moving Sqij about a bit, the screen is a mess of virtual bird droppings as the graphics corrupt.

scrawl while a number increases.

The problem is the game's code forces caps lock to stay on, but it then only accepts lower case key inputs. Apparently "playtesting" and "quality control" were terms totally missing in whatever alien language The Power House understood. And not only did they release the game in this state, they released it twice – first on its own, and then as part of a compilation.

However! Due to the monstrous, cosmic-level ineptitude of the programming, the BREAK key has not been disabled, so you can dive right into the source code and alter it at whim after pressing a single button. Also, the memory contains the full binaries for Laser Basic, the language the game was programmed in, meaning it effectively contains a pirate copy of a £14.99 utility. This is why testing a game before putting it on shelves and charging people for it is a good idea. So, by stopping the program and switching off caps lock in the memory (That's POKE 23658,0 if you want to try this at home) you can actually play *SQIJ!*

But then things get even worse. Animation is entirely limited to a small spasm on the row of dots representing Sqij's wing. There is no sound other

```
   1 GO TO 2
   3 PAPER 0: CLS : BEEP 0.1,34:
LET opt=0: LET o=0: INK 7: LET
x=0: LET y=1: LET p=1: LET paz=0
: LET u=10: LET lo=0: BEEP 0.1,9
: BORDER 0: BEEP .2,45
   6 LET kl=0: LET ob=0: LET sc=
0: LET trc=0: LET pas=0: LET tre
e=0: LET food=0: LET room=29: LE
T d1=0: LET d2=0: LET d3=0: LET
d4=0: LET d5=0: LET d6=0
   7 LET obj3=0: LET obj4=0: LET
 obj5=0: LET obj6=0: LET obj7=0:
 LET obj8=0: LET obj9=0: LET obj
10=0: LET obj11=0: LET obj12=0:
LET obj13=0: LET obj14=0: LET ob
j15=0: LET obj16=0: LET r=0
   8 LET d3=0: LET d4=0: LET d5=
0: LET d6=0: LET xc=0: LET ro=0
   9 LET z=0: LET left=0: LET ri
ght=0: LET up=0: LET down=0
  10 LET obj1=0: LET obj2=0: LET
POKE 23658,0
```

The start of the source code. Notice that line 1 exists solely to point to line 2. A ridiculous redundancy. Now notice that line 2 doesn't exist.

than a few random beeps when the game loads. The instructions list eight control keys but only four seem to do anything at first, and they are the ones that move you around the screen. Sqij flickers and jerks in a direction if you hold it down long enough. The scribble enemies move at a glacial pace and stop moving when you do. Graphic glitches are rife – as you move you leave weird trails and can actually tear parts off the scribbles if you go near them. And ultimately playing the game seems futile as any attempt to leave the middle of the screen bounces poor Sqij back and costs him ten energy points. It doesn't matter if you're near an enemy or not; there's no escape.

But! Whilst pressing the shoot button seemingly does nothing, if you're aligned with a certain part of an enemy it disappears with no visual or audio feedback, and you can leave the room. If your patience is infinite then you can move farcically slowly around the map and get to the end and save the world or whatever. As an additional irritant, you often appear at the wrong entrance when you enter a room – enter it from the right and you'll appear at the bottom, etc.

Of course *SQIJ!* isn't the only game to have been released broken, bug-ridden and incomplete. C-Tech's *Krazy Kong* for the Spectrum was so infamously poor that *Computer and Video Games* magazine dedicated an entire page to readers' complaints about it. But *SQIJ!* is the most egregious example I've come across.

By far the best thing about the game is the cover art, which is a shame as it may have enticed people to buy it. The Power House often reused existing art, and this striking, dynamic image of a mutant bat by Tim White is a beautiful example. It was painted for the cover of the 1975 sci-fi novel *Under a Calculating Star* by John Morressy, and it has been used for multiple books since. The screenshots shown on the back of the cassette were from the Commodore 64 version with a note saying "Screen shots may vary from your version", presumably in order to hide the visual horror of the actual version you were buying.

And *SQIJ!* just doesn't stop giving! At the time of release, The Power House were adding free audio tracks

A scan of my copy of SQIJ! Yes, I paid money for it. Pity me.

to their cassettes after the game data. They were promoting the music of a band called H.E.X. (House Electronic Xperience). Presumably they were connected to them in some way. The song on the *SQIJ!* tape is a repetitive, five minute funk track with semi-audible vocals that sounds like it was recorded on an old tape recorder in a bathroom. There's no title given, but from what I can make out of the lyrics, it's called something like *Swimming Against the Tide of the Time.*

So what the hell does *SQIJ!* mean anyway? Professional video gaming man Larry Bundy Jr suggested to

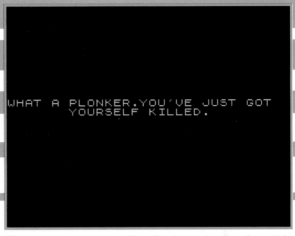

The game over screen, adding insult to already substantial injury.

me that it's a corruption of squigeon, a colloquial term for a pigeon. As the game stars a bird, I think that's by far the most likely explanation. It annoys me that there's no U after the Q though, as the English language doesn't work like that.

SQIJ! was written by Jason Creighton, who actually supplied an explanation for the game's startling lack of quality on the Spectrum 2.0 review website. Apparently he was

contractually obligated by The Power House to produce the game, but after he fell out with a member of staff, he didn't want to deliver it. After avoiding the issue for a while, he wrote a deliberately terrible game in 40 hours to get them off his back, understanding that they would reject it. But as we all know, they happily duplicated it and sent it off to shops instead.

He also claimed that the caps lock error wasn't in the original game, and

The Power House included digitised photos of programmers in their cassette inlays. Mr Creighton does not appear to be amused.

that it's possibly caused by modern computers emulating the Spectrum's hardware. I can debunk that immediately – I've played an original copy of the game on both a 48K+ and a 128K+2, and the caps lock error absolutely is present. Maybe it wasn't in the version he sent to The Power House and they added it? Seems unlikely as I very much doubt they paid any attention to it after checking that it loaded up, or they would never have released it...

A look at the source code for the game reveals not only a frightening number of internal variables that don't do anything, but a message to be displayed if the impossible happens and the game is completed. It reads: "WELL DONE OLD BEAN!! YOU'VE DONE IT. BUT FOR ME IT MEANS ANOTHER 2 MONTHS IN A DARK DANK BEDROOM (WHICH BADLY NEEDS DECORATING) WRITEING A FOLLOW UP. OH WELL. NEVER MIND. BYE FOR NOW." The glamourous world of the bedroom coder hasn't changed much in 30 years.

Although almost unknown at the time, *SQIJ!* has gone on to garner infamy in the Spectrum community. The annual comp.sys.sinclair crap games competition, where people write deliberately awful Spectrum games, is currently hosted at sqij.co.uk. There could be no more fitting tribute.

REVIEW SCORES

No known reviews.

OTHER VERSIONS

Commodore 64: This original version is predictably completely different. It's a smooth, well-animated exploration game with heavy shoot 'em up elements. The bad news is that it's frustrating rubbish – your energy drains away so quickly that most games last less than a minute, and most deaths are caused by getting caught on the background when you enter a new screen. The music is nice, though.

Commodore 16: Wow. This conversion could be an entry into this book on its own merits... or lack thereof. Similar to the C64 version and just as smooth, the positives end there. It's insanely fast, Sqij looks like an apple, every screen has the same weird chain of portraits flying around it, you can't kill anything so your bullets are useless, and there's no sound. Not as frustrating as the C64 version, but worse as a game.

The Commodore 64 version. Looks like a prototype of Angry Birds.

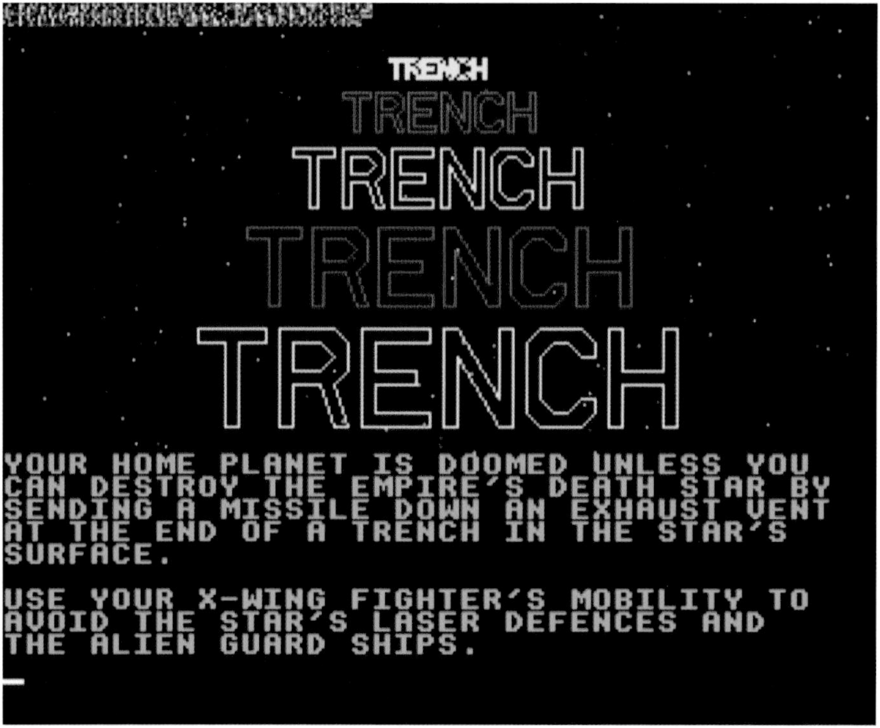

TRENCH
TRENCH
TRENCH
TRENCH
TRENCH
YOUR HOME PLANET IS DOOMED UNLESS YOU CAN DESTROY THE EMPIRE'S DEATH STAR BY SENDING A MISSILE DOWN AN EXHAUST VENT AT THE END OF A TRENCH IN THE STAR'S SURFACE.
USE YOUR X-WING FIGHTER'S MOBILITY TO AVOID THE STAR'S LASER DEFENCES AND THE ALIEN GUARD SHIPS.

TRENCH

FORMAT: BBC MICRO
YEAR OF RELEASE: 1983
DEVELOPER: UNKNOWN
PUBLISHER: VIRGIN GAMES
ORIGINAL PRICE: 7.99 POUNDS

A laser blast narrowly misses the X-wing fighter! Not that the player had any say in the matter.

THE CLIMACTIC DEATH STAR trench battle in *Star Wars* is one of the most iconic sequences in cinema. Everyone remembers the exhilaration of watching Luke Skywalker skim along the battle station's surface as half of his friends blew up around him, then seeing him turn off his targeting computer because he heard a dead man's voice. The makers of *Trench* were obviously fans too, as they shamelessly ripped it off for this game. *Trench* doesn't attempt to hide its influences. It specifically refers to "the Empire's Death Star" and "your X-wing fighter" in the instructions, although oddly it refers to TIE fighters as "alien guard ships." The setup is exactly as you would expect – you have to fly along a trench and then shoot an exhaust port the size of a womp rat to blow up the Death Star.

First impressions are extremely positive. The game starts with a rear view of your fighter flying into the trench as laser blasts hit the walls around you. In the background are constant whooshing noises and the pew-pew of the lasers. Then a siren-like sound starts as a TIE fighter comes flying towards you – it's genuinely exciting as you feel like you've been thrown into the middle of the action, yet it's still easy to take

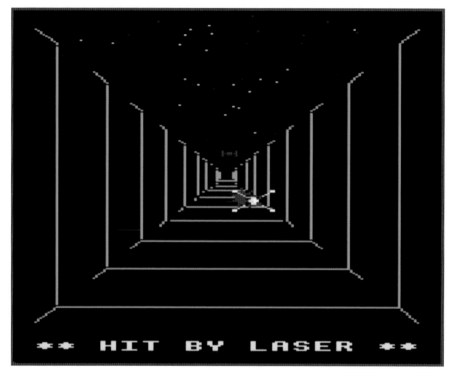

And that's it – the game is over. And to think they painted that TIE fighter red for nothing.

stock of what's going on around you. Then one of the lasers hits you and it's instantly game over, even though you've only been playing for a few seconds. Surprised, you wonder what happened. You start the game again

Whoops. Sorry everyone!

and your second impressions are an awful lot less positive. The hideous, Grand Canyon-sized flaws in the game design become obvious as soon as you fully get your bearings. The first flaw is a disappointment – despite there being a button for "shoot", you cannot attack the TIE fighters. You only have a single shot saved for the exhaust port at the end.

The second flaw utterly cripples the game: the lasers that shoot into the trench appear instantly and at random in the rough area your ship is in. There is zero indication of where they're coming from and as such they are literally impossible to dodge. All you can do is move around and hope that one doesn't appear on top of you, meaning the game is down to luck rather than skill. And, of course, you have no extra lives, so the slightest hit ends the game immediately.

Other exciting ways to die include hitting one of the TIE fighters that jerk towards you or moving to the extreme edges of the screen where you hit the trench walls. Even travelling to the very top of the screen is enough to end the game, as apparently going "out of trench" invokes an immediate death penalty.

If the *Trench* gods are on your side, you may survive the short flight to the exhaust point. Here the game switches to a first-person view, showing the

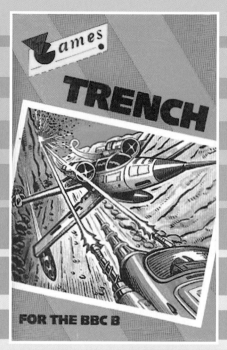

No, Mister Copyright Lawyer. That's definitely not an X-wing fighter. Not at all.

exhaust port as a 3D environment made up of a few lines. It runs at about three frames a second, so to say control at this point is sluggish would possibly be the biggest understatement of

the century so far. You have to position the tiny port – which inexplicably doesn't get larger the closer you get to it – right in the centre of your targeting reticule before you fire. Your ship is glacially slow in this stage, so it takes ages to line up, and you can only just get a shot in before you smack into the trench wall in front of you. Hit it dead on and – you've guessed it! – you still continue onwards and smack into the wall. The "Game Over" message states, "You have destroyed the Empire's Death Star, but at the loss of your own life." I suppose it may be possible to escape in the handful of movement frames left, but I've not come close to working out how.

Trench is one of the most frustrating games I've ever played. But if that irritation isn't enough for you, the difficulty level can be cranked up, which increases the frequency of the laser blasts and thus the likelihood of instantly losing the game due to circumstances utterly beyond your control.

REVIEW SCORES

None. The only reference I could find to Trench anywhere in a magazine was an advert selling it in January 1984, which is why I've assumed a release date of sometime in 1983.

OTHER VERSIONS

None. Just play Death Star Interceptor on the ZX Spectrum instead, as it takes the same basic idea, but the outcome is actually based on some measure of skill rather than blind luck.

THE MOST DISAPPOINTING GAME I EVER BOUGHT

BY VIOLET BERLIN, WHO MADE
TV SHOWS ABOUT GAMES IN THE
NINETIES AND THE NORTIES,
AND IS NOW A SCRIPTWRITER FOR
GAMES & OTHER INTERACTIVE MEDIA

CASTLEVANIA II: SIMON'S QUEST
FORMAT: NINTENDO ENTERTAINMENT SYSTEM
YEAR OF RELEASE: 1987 (1990 UK)
DEVELOPER: KONAMI
PUBLISHER: KONAMI
ORIGINAL PRICE: APPROX. 34.99 POUNDS

I LOVED the first Castlevania *on NES. Sooo much. I went hours and hours saying "just one more go", unable to stop playing, faint from hunger, and staying up all night.*

Then Castlevania II *came out. Reviewers loved its genre-breaking boldness – it introduced RPG elements and cryptic clues. Amazing! Except that the clues were too cryptic, or even non-existent in some puzzles, and I now know that subtleties lost in the English translation were partly to blame.*

Castlevania II *was a closed book to me. Or, rather, it was an exciting book that wouldn't open. Today you can just go on the net and find a walkthrough. Not so in those days. I was the only person I knew who played video games, so I was out in the cold with this one.*

Reading about Castlevania II *now, with hindsight, it is acknowledged that it didn't give proper clues, and without a walkthrough, it was almost impossible to know what to do. Apparently there was*

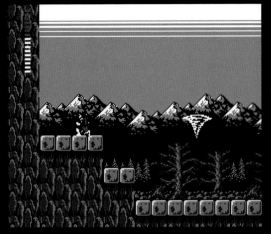

one in Nintendo Power *magazine
back in the day, but I didn't see it.*
So even though Castlevania II
*had great promise, it was actually
a mean trick... an impossible game
that the reviewers probably got
help with. The screen I was stuck on
is still burnt into my memory, and I
didn't play any* Castlevania *games
after that.*

You can find Violet on Twitter at
@VioletBerlin

FACT!

The most infamously opaque
puzzle in *Castlevania II* involves
the following two clues: "HIT
DEBORAH CLIFF WITH YOUR
HEAD TO MAKE A HOLE" and
"WAIT FOR A SOUL WITH A RED
CRYSTAL ON DEBORAH CLIFF".
What you actually have to do is
kneel down in a specific place
after equipping yourself with a
red crystal and wait a few seconds, at which point a tornado
takes you further into the game.
Unbelievable. The infinitely
clearer Japanese version of the
second clue states "PRESENT
THE RED CRYSTAL IN FRONT
OF DEBORAH'S CLIFF AND WAIT
FOR THE WIND", which implies
that the translation was completed by a partially concussed
nitwit.

ACKNOWLEDGEMENTS

I would like to offer thanks and appreciation to:

- Mike Cook, without whom this book would not exist.
- The team at Unbound for all their work and believing in this book in the first place.
- ChinnyHill10 for kindly checking that I hadn't messed up the technical details of the Amstrad CPC.
- Sarah Watts for her useful advice on equestrian matters.
- Brad Taylor, who independently confirmed my research into Sam Coupé games only for none of the information to be used... yet.
- The unknown army of people who scan old video game magazines and upload them to the Internet.
- People who watch my YouTube videos, as without them I'd have nothing. And that would be rubbish.

INDEX

TERRIBLE NAMES YOU'VE PROBABLY NEVER HEARD OF

Unbound is the world's first crowdfunding publisher, established in 2011.

We believe that wonderful things can happen when you clear a path for people who share a passion. That's why we've built a platform that brings together readers and authors to crowdfund books they believe in – and give fresh ideas that don't fit the traditional mould the chance they deserve.

This book is in your hands because readers made it possible. Everyone who pledged their support is listed below. Join them by visiting unbound.com and supporting a book today.

A frankly absurdly large
amount of tat

A tiny Asian man with 17
Welsh sex slaves

"An Excellent Bryan
Goldsmith"

AnthonyGiants
AnthonyGiants

Akwa

BADMAN 2

The Baryshnikov Twins

Big Hairy Marty

Brandon and Becky

[CITATION NEEDED]

Dom and Faye

GameGlitchGuy G3

Geoffrey, The Meownarch of
Kittenia

[INSERT NAME HERE]

Jonathan May, loves Hailey,
Buddy, and Mishu

Lara S and Lissy H

Mackenzie & Yivo

Michael Kitch and Sam
Clements

Most evil bastard

R M.

Vicky and Craig

Jack Abbott

Loren Abbott

Markel Abel

Adrian Acosta

Jake Adams

Peter Adams

Ronni Adams

Slater Adams

Terry Adams

Anakin Adcock

John Adlington

Angela Adrian

Aaliyah Agar

Joshua Agar

Anthony Aggett

Michael Agostinelli

Alice Ahn

Simon Aitken

Neil Aitken

Kim Akerø

David Alasow

Robert Alavoine

Oskar "Shamelessly asking
if you ever used a BBS?"
Albinsson

António Albuquerque

Adam Alby

Cody Alcina

Jaber Al-Eidan

Andréa Alexander

Andrew "imnotanerd" Scott
Ali

Ediz Ali

Brian Allan

James Allan

Greg Allen

Paul Allen

Jim Alm

Mariah Almeida

Robert Altoft

Jose Alvarez

Vasco Alves

Matthew Amann

Emma Amfelt

Arman "Eyebro" Amin

Mike Amos

Justin Anastasio

Brad Anderson

Craig "Fox" Anderson

Stephanie Anderson

Virginia Anderson

Will Anderson

Cayden Andrews

Chris Andrews

Frankie Andrews

Tova Äng

Christian Ankerstjerne

Alexander Answine

David Anthony

Omari "Techandtrains101"
Antony

Oskari Anttalainen

Drake Anubis

Nathan Applegarth

Phil Arber

Peter Arbuthnot

Guillem Arias

Alex Aris

Chris Arlott

Chris Armitage

Tom Armstrong

Dan Arries

Elliot Ash

Elizabeth Ashford

Dominic Ashman

Jason Ashmore

Tharglet Asimis

Magnus Asplund

Hannah Atkins

Nick Atkins

Michael Atkinson

Troy Atkinson

Tom Austin

Paul Auton

Jessica Ayako

Michael Ayling

Lady Azkadelia

Collin Bachman

Nicholas Backhouse

Erica Bäcklund

Calyb Badger

Jordan Badger

Doctor Bag PhD

Lewis Bage

James Bagg

Richard Baggaley

Paul Baggett

Andrew Bailey

Chris Bailey

Logan Bailey

Michael Bailey

Richard J Bailey

Richard Bairwell

Connor Baker

Josh Baker

Matthew Baker

Mike Baker

Vyvyen Baker

Dustin Baldus

Joe Baldwin

Stephen Baldwin

Jamie Balfour

Christopher Ball

Mark Ball

Matthew Ball

Kyle Ballagher

Robin Ballard

Toby Balshaw

Russ Bamber

Andrew Banas

Jack Bannerman

Broderic Banta

Adam Barbery

Jennifer Barden

Andre Bardin

Nik "TFk" Barham

Toby Barham

Matthew Barhorst

Andrius Barkauskas

Ryan Barkham

Riyad Barmania

Patrick Barnes

Tony Barnett

Jakob Barnstorf

Danielle Barr

Emma Barratt

Dane Barrett

Darrell Barrett

Joe Barrett

James Barry

Elliot Bartram

Jeremy Baruffa

Arnold Bashkevits

Paul Bastin

Jean Batzloff

Gavin Bauer

Daniel Baxendale

Chris Baxter

Chelsi Beale

Sheree Beasley

Fraser Beattie

Connor Beck

Greg Beck

Joseph F. Becker

John Beckett

Richard Beckett

Matthew Beckly

Michael Bedra

Daniel Beeley

Robyn Behan

Michael Behle

Keir Beigel

Aaron Bekir

Ole Bekkelund

Adrian Belcher

Andrew Bell

David Bell

Erik Bell

Mark Bell

Michael Bell

Philip Bell

Paul Bellamy

Christopher Belt

Garry Benfold

Kristoffer Bengtsson

Charles Bennett

Jon Bennett

Scott Bennett

Stan Bennett

Alex Bentley

Boris Bentley

Joe Bentley

Jon Bentley
Jared Berga
Lars Berge
Sven Berghuijs
Robert P. Bergman
CJ Berrisford
Michael Berry
Patrick Berry
Sam Berry
Simon Berry
Tim Berry
Koen Bertels
Leonardo Bertinelli
Chris Beshansky
Tim Best
Owain Bestley
Tom Betts
Kent Bevan
Sam Bevan
Sabrina Bewey
Christopher Bezzina
Braeden Bice
Eric Bickerdyke
Marcel Bienert
Jordan Bigness
Matthew Billany
Sophie Billing
David Bilous
Charlotte Birch
Jordan Bird
David Birdsall
Alexander Birk
Nicholas Birlie
Aidan Bishop
Scott Bishop

Isaac Bishop-Ponte
Joshua Bitzer
Jostein Bjørge
Guy Black
Robin Black
Tryston Black
Zayne Black
Robert Blackburn
Tom Blackburn
Craig S. Blackie
Alex Blackmon
Hugo Blair
Emily Blance
Andrew Blane
Elana Blane
Stephen Blane
Thomas Blindbaek
Jonathan Bloom
Nathan Bloomfield
Jürgen Bloß
Martyn Blundell
Alan Blyth
Kim Blyth
Tabitha Bodin
Philipp Boehme
Ed Boff
Bartek Bok
Steve Bolsover
Graeme Bolton
Jason Bonar
Jack Daniel Bond
Wilf Bond
Nicolai Bonde
David Bone
Anthony Bonica

Cees Bood
Anthony Booth
James Booth
Kevin Booth
Matt Booth
Robert Booth
Tim Boring
Victoria Borisova
Reese Borowiak
James Borrett
Scott Boughton
Hakim Boukellif
Alan Boulais
Chris Boulton
James Bouma
Joel Bourassa
William Bourgeois
Antoine Bourget
George Bourne
Nicola Bourne
Mackinnon Bowden
James Bowen
Drew Bower
Bodhi Bowers
Adam Bowes
Luke Bowes
Joth Bowgett
James Bowman
Munroe Stephen Stanley
    Box-Cameron
Jacob Boyce
Bethany Boyd
David Boyd
Sean Frederick Boynton
Jacob Bracken

Graham Bradbury
Donya Bradshaw
James Bradshaw
Mark Bradshaw -
  (QuantumParadox)
Owen Brady
Paul Braiden
Christopher Brailsford
Dave Brain
William Brall
Tyler Bramley
Ewan Brammall
Kristen Brand
Michael Brand
Lee Brandon
Claus Just Brandstrup
Asbjørn Brask
Alex Breach
Derek Brealey
Martin Brear
Joshua Breazeale
Jamie Breeze
William Breeze
Mike Brent
Tom Brent
Simon William Brett
Wyatt Brewer
Dino Brewster
Alex Bricault
Roy Brickey
Ian Bridge
Billy Bridgeman
Timothy Bridges
Mat Brignall
William Brittain

Alice Broadribb
Johan Brockstedt
Louis Bromilow
Martin Brook
Matt Brook
Sam Brookes
Tim Brookes
Chris Brooks
Shaun "Dave" Brooks
Josh Broom
Brendan Brothers
Adam Brough
Ryan "madspy" Browell
Andrew Brown
Antony Brown
Austen Brown
Carl Brown
Dan M Brown
Ethan Macnair Brown
Gary Brown
George Brown
Graham Brown
Kevin Brown
Louise Brown
Stuart Brown
Theodore Brown
Zachary Brown
Carly Browne
Olly Browning
Phil Bruce-Moore
Carine Brunet
Max Bruton
Steve Bryce
Michael Buchan (Squeeowl)
Robert Buchan

Rosie Buck
Kevin Bucknall
Hendri Budi
David Budziszewski
Lars Bull
Sam Bull
Matthew Bulley
Andrew Bullock
Stuart Bullock
Stephen Bunclark
Kirk Bunston
Antonio M. Buonomo
Ian Matthew Burch
Martin C Burchett
Wes Burden
Ethan Burge
Calum Burgess
Matthew Burke
Alex Burnett
Andrew Burnett
Ross Burnett
Stephanie Burnette
Daniel Burridge
Kyle Burrows
Peter Burrows
Grant Burt
Richard Burton
Joe Bussert
Ben Butcher - JedForces
Anthony Butirro
Lee Butler
Alicia Butteriss
Robert Butterworth
Alan Byrne
Elizabeth Byrne

Thomas Byrne
Scott Byrne-Fraser
Kale Cabbage
Alejandro Cabrera
Stephen Caile
Pete Cain
Liam Caldwell
Aaron Calhoun
Ryan Callaghan
Tim Callaghan
Robert Callister
Craig Cameron
Scott "Young Scott" Cameron
Harry Campbell
Andy & Joy Candler
Rachel Cann
Daniel Capaldi
Rob Caporetto
Mark Carbonaro
Dane Carless
Philip Carlson
Rachel Carn
Manuel Gomez Carnero
Gavin S Carpenter
Louise Carpenter
Mark Carr
Matthew Carr
Nicholas Carr
David J. Carreiro
Tom Carrick
Bryan Carroll
David Carruthers
Stuart Carruthers
Seth Carson
Dan Carter

Laurie Carter
Alex Cartwright
Alice Casey
Karla Castillo
Mark Caswell
Caution Cat
Tenshi Cat
Corey Catalano
Gregory Cathcart
Richard Caywood
Josh (Yimyams) Chablis
Jean-Baptiste Chabrier
Barnaby Chambers
Gary Chambers
Scott Chambers
Tom Chamley
Chris Chan
Kai Chance
Ben Chandler
Edward Chapman
Harry Chapman
James Chapman
Jordan Charles
Sam Charleston
Ben Charlesworth
Rohan Charlseworth
Rory Charlesworth
Cameron Charlton
Philip Charlton
Steven Charlton
Alexander Chase
Tom Chatham
Tom Chatt
James Chatterton
Isaiah Chavez

Jon Cheng
Joseph Cherrett
Alexander Blake Cheskis
Alex Chesnut
Jordan Chew
Chloe Cheyne
Joseph Chiappa
Luke Childs
Ameya Chilekar
David Chipres
Andy Chirnside
Johannes Christ
Rasmus Mejer Christensen
Gordon Chung
Richard Churchill
Steven M. F. X. Cimprich
Daniel Clackson
Reed Clanton
Ben Clark
Em Clark
James Clark
Kieran Clark
Lewis Clark
Matthew Clark
McKay Clark
Ben Clarke
Iwan Clarke
Kieran Clarke
Matthew "DK" Clarke
Scott Clarke
Steven Clarke
Toby Claus
Joe Clausen
Brennan Clay
Joe Clay

David Clearwater
Tom Cleaver
Lachlan Clement
Scott Clements
Sean Clements
Jordan Cleverley
Josh Cliff
Robert Cliffe
Shane Cloherty
Josh Close
Jessica Clossey
Stuart Clough
Garrett Coakley
Nick Coakley
Richard Cobbett
Jay Cochran
Andrew Coggin
Macauley Coggins
Thomas Cohen
Maxime Cohin
Mario Coiro
Darren Colclough
Benjamin Cole
Christine Cole
Rhiannon Coleman
Nathan Collen
Shaun Collier
Christopher Collingridge
James Collins
Timothy Collins
Murray Colpman
Lily-May Colson
Ben Condon
Callum Connah
Rory Conneely

Christopher Connor
M. Conrace
Evan Conrod
Ryan Constantin
Freaky Constantina
Fatim Conteh
Conall W M Conway
Ashley Cook
Caleb Cook
Jamie Cook
Jessie Cook
Nicholas Cook
Ollie Cook
Sam Cook
Andrew Cooke
Jack Cooper
James Cooper
Joe Cooper
Neil Cooper
Richard Cooper
Richard W Cooper
Taylor Cooper
Tim Cooper
Zachary Cooper
Mike Coopland
Mark Cope
Michael Coppolino
Paul Corkindale
Michael Cormier
Brenton Costan
Alec Costan
Andrew Costin
Amanda Cournoyer
Aaron Coville
Matthew Cowan

Jack Coward
Scott Cowie
Eleri Cowlyn
Daniel Cox
Kieran Cox
Leon Cox
Lewis Cox
Matthew Alexander Cox
Sam Coy
Kit Coyne
Rebecca Crabb
Danielle Crain
Elizabeth Crampin
Matthew Crane
James Cranwell
Mike Crawford
Joel Cresswell
Kane Crichton
Bram Crielaard
Philip Crisp
Magnus Criwall
Kyle Crocker
Mihai Catalin Croicu
Mark Crook
Matthew Crook
Mark Crosby
Terry Crosher
Alex Crossley
Rob Crossley
Johnston Crothers
Ben Crowe
Adam Crowell
Matt Crowhurst
Richard Crowther
Aaron Crutchley

Gabriel Cruz
Christopher Csabon
Sanya Culp
Jake Culshaw
John Culverhouse
Curtis Cummings
Luke Cummins
Mallory Currier
James Curry
Simon Curry
Tom Curtis
Kelsey Custodio
Chris Cutts
Sarah Louise Cutts
Daniel D'Abate
Peter Daisley
Sandy Dakers
Sebastian Dalby
David Dalcino
Laura Dale
Stuart Dales
Daniel Daley
Dave Daniels
Thomas Lee Darby
Julian Daugaard
Craig Daveson
Daragh Davey
Colin Davidson
Sam Davidson
Adam Davies
Kyea Davies
Mark Davies
Matthew Davies
Paul "Wid3boy" Davies
Stu & Lindz Davies

Tony Davies
Adam Davis
Alex Davis
Jacob "Davistoa" Davis
Michael Davis
Morgan "Mo" Davis
Sam Davis
Adrian Davison
Allan Davison
Richard Davison
Samuel Dawes
Kayleigh Dawson
Mark Dawson
Harry de Carle
Danny De Casto
Dik de Jong
Cas de Rooij
Martin Dean
Shaban Jonathan Dean
Tobias Dean
Elliot Deans
Devin Debenport
Aaron Deicmanis
Jürgen Deinlein
Kayla and Zachary Del Rio
Niall Delaney
Stephen DeLay
Chris DelGobbo
Lee Dellbridge
Joe Demartino
Adam Demmon
Sophia & Joe Dempsey
Mark Dempster
Jack Denham
Thomas Obi Denham

Jenny Denholm
Christopher Denk
Matthew Denning
Kyle Dennis
Matthew Dent
Jonathan Denton
Wyatt Denues
Corey Derbyshire
Ryan Dermody
Ian Derrick
Tim Dettmar
Sebastian Deußer
Devjock Devjock
Lukas DeVries
Félix Dewaleyne
Corey DeWalt
Emily Diamond
Nathan Dibley
Stuart Anderson Dick
Miranda Dickinson
Stuart Dickinson
Jens Dietrich
Kevyn Dietz
Gabriel DiGennaro
Brendon Robert Dillon
Jude Dillon
Jonny Dimaline
Matthew Dimmick
Simon Dimmock
Thomas "Dimmock" Johnson
Sean DiMuzio
Sasha Distan
Thom Divine
Adam Dixon
Jono Dixon

Sarah Dixon
James Dobson
Terry Doel
Adam Doheny
Chris Doig
Sebastian Domagala
Jack Domenici
Jacob Donaghy
Ethan Donnachie
Kevin Donnellon
Amy Donnelly
Claire Baker Donnelly
Robert Donovan
Christian Doran
Sarah Dorrington
Jack Dorris
Anthony D'Orsi
Christopher Dostal
Aaron Doughty of Amigos
    Podcast
Joshua Dowding
Craig Downer
Thomas Downes
Andrew Doyle
Connor Doyle
Hannah Doyle
Jean-Raphaël Doyon
Thomas Drake
Laurent Dreikaus
Nicholas Drew
Thomas Drinan
Kirill Dronov
Colin Drum
Christopher Dudley
Cormac Duffy

Sean Dugan
Eric "Carrot" Skylar Duncan
John Duncan
Alex Dunn
Michael Dunn
Richard Dunn
Ryan Dunn
Scott Dunn
Vivienne Dunstan
Steven Duong
Andrew Durney
Hog Duske
Neil Dutton
Gary DuVall
Graeme Dyas
Rainer Dybevick
Doug Dysart
Liam Earley
Logan Eason
Peter East
Beverley Eastwood
Owen Eastwood
Josh Eaton
Will Eaton
Tom Eatwell
Daniel Eccleston
Richard Eckley
James Edge
Pete Edge
Timothy Edmonds
Christian Edwards
Edward Edwards
John Edwards - "An Excellent
    Bloke"
John Edwards

Kelman Edwards
Stephen Edwards
Tom Edwards
David Eggleton
Harry Egre
Nathan Ehrlich
Jake Ehuan
Jack Eisenmann
Adam Eisenstein
Greg Ekstrom
Dominick Elio
Aidan Ellams
Matthew Ellerington
Addam Ellington-Lewis
Thomas Ellinson
Ariel Elliott
Daniel Elliott
Chris Ellis
David Ellis
Morgan Ellis
Paul Ellis
Peyton Ellis
Richard Ellis
Sadie Ellis
David Ellwood
Scott Elrick
Rob Wagner Else
Timothy Elsy
Vidar Viking Elvigen
Galen Embry
Harry Emmott
Marshall Eng
Marius Engen
Paul England
Edward Englund

EpicLPer EpicLPer
Wolfgang Christopher Arispe
   Ervin
Matthew Etherington
Ryan Etherington
Alex Evans
Calum Evans
Daniel Evans
Edward Evans
Euan Euan
Graham Evans
Morgan Evans
Neil Evans
Paul Evans
Stuart Evans
Terry Evans
Harry Evely
Matthew Evert
Patrick Evison
Duncan Ewart
Paul Fadness
Benjamin Faiers
Chris Faiers
Sapphire Fairhurst
Robert Falb
Paul Fallon
Edwin Falter
Thomas Faltermeier
Antoine Fantys
Jacob Farrimond
Daniel Fawcett
James Fellows
Paddy Fellows
Christopher Femalè
Matt Ferguson

Daniel Fern
Erik Fernsund
David (mightyferret) Ferries
Thomas Ferry
Heather-Louise Fewins
Robert Fiddis
Chris Field
James Fielden
Richard Fielding
Lia Filippone
Casey Finder
Bret Finley
Luke Finnegan
Nicola R. Fiorelli
Joe Firman
Nick Firth
Andrew Fisher
Joseph Fishlock
Austin Fitch
Richard Fitzjohn
Michael Flack
V. Flack
Adam Flaxman
Katya M R P Fleming
Jack Fletcher
Josh Fletcher
Cameron Gazorpazorp
   fleuchar
Joseph Flint
Jorge Flores
Matthew Floyd
Jake Floyd-Eve
Dean Flukes
Peter Fodor
Paul Fogarty

Marc Fokkert
Emily Forbes
Adam Ford
Christopher Ford
Steve Ford
David Fornuff
Mike Forrest
Jamie Forsyth
William Forsyth
Emma Foster
John Foster
Stacey Foster
Geoffrey Fountain
Allan Fouracre
Vincent Fournier
Ben Fox
Josh Fox
Tim Foxall
Sebastian Fraatz
Kelsey Frame
Dan France
Philip France
Josh Francis
Lorenzo Francis
Monika Francis
Andrew Franklin
Samuel Franklin
Thomas Franklin
Finlay Franks
Aaron Franz
David Franzkoch
Joshua Fraser
Lachlan Fraser
Stuart "Felix" Fraser
Cameron Fray

Jens Fredriksson
Jeremy Free
Mike Freeman
Games Freezer
Max Freshour
Colby Friend
Theo Friess
Þór Friggjarkind
Carl Frill
Garry Fromont
Torey Frost
James Fry
Ian Fuller
Robert Fultz
Karsing Fung
Garry Furey
Justin Furlong
Axel Furzer
Cameron Gable
John Gabriel
Charlie Gadd
Matthias Gaebel
Sam Gain
Joseph Gaiser
James Gale
Shaun Gale
Anna Gales
Jake Patrick Gallagher
Rachael Galley
Mark Gamble
GameNeek GameNeek
Nicholas Gammans
Liam Francis Gannon
Ian Garcia
Barry Gardiner

Jonny Gardiner
Jordan Gardiner
Robert Gardiner
Ed Gardner
Steve "Xevian" Gare
Mike Garland
Ian Garner
William Garrard
Billy Garratt-John
Michael "Mikki" Garry
Daniel "Lord-Ashford" Garton
Edward Gaudion
Ashley Gaul
Dmitriy Gavryushkin
David Gaynor
Melanie Geer
Alex Geeves
Mariah Geiger
Andrew Gelhard
Max Gent
Daniel Geoghan
Nils Georgii
Jack Gerard
Michael Gernoth
Sebastian Gerstl
Jan Geselle
Sol Getcheffsky
Marius Ghita
Harry Gibb
Leon Gibb
Douglas Gibbons
Mark Gibbons
Scott Gibbs
Frederick Gibson
Carl Gietl

Andrew Gilbert
Christopher Gilbert
Neil Gilbert
Peter Thomas Gildersleve
Ben Gill
Travis Gillett
Isaiah Gillette
Billy Giorgio
Adam Girling
Nigel Henryk Girouard
Jon Gjelle
Lewis Glaister
Ed Glaser
James Glass
David Glover
James Glover
David Glover-Aoki
Jack Gloyens
Adam Glynn
Danny Godál
Peter Godden
Jose Godoi
Steve Godrich
Killian Goetowski
Christopher Goldasz
David Gometz
Dennis Gooden
Sean Goodliffe
Max Goodman
Andrew Goodro
Dan Goodwin
James Goral
Zack Gordon
Vijay Kumar Goswami
Tim Goss

Tom Gothorp
Ben Gough (Terrum)
Chris "Chairs" Gough
Alex Gould
Archie Gould
Gemma Gould
Andrew Goulding
Jack Gowrie
Nick Grabau
Jamie Graham
Tim Grainger
Callum Grant
Joe Grant
Xiola Granville
Joanne Grason
Troy Grauel
Jon Graves
Adam Gray
Callum Gray
Joshua Gray
Matt Greaves
Ben Green
Chris Green
Mark Green
Spencer Green
Walter Green
Rachael Greenfield
James E Greenhorn
Mark Greenwood
Wayne "Greeny" Greenwood
Mikkel Gregersen
Phoebe Greggor
Micheal Gregory
Harry Gregory
Stuart Greig

Matthew Greig
Mark Griffin
Nathan Griffin
Phillip Griffin
Mike Griffiths
Christopher Grimshaw
Jai Grimshaw
Frank Grisi
Edward John Gizzi
Brett Grocke
William Groom
Andrew Grover
Tom Groves
John Grun
Shauni Grund
Simon Grundy
Antoni Guest
Fu Gui
Chris Guler
Andrew Gurcsik
Mike Gurval
Catalina Gutierrez
Benjamin Guy
Carl Guyton
Davis Gysin
James Habermann
Jenny Hackett
Tre Had
Russell Haddock
Reece Hagan
Joshua Hagon-Fenton
Evan SirFucknut Haines
Ilja Häkkinen
Ed Hale
Thomas Hale

Simon Hales
Graham Hall
Jarrett Hall
Rhiannon Davies Hall
Kelvin Ham
Ben Hames
Steven Hamilton
Philip Hamling
Andreas Schack Hammann
Katie Hammer
Sam Hampshire
Stephen Hampshire
Youssef and Yara Hamway
Ashley Hancock
Christopher Hancock
Emma Hancock
Kieran Hancock
Richard Hancock
Matt Hancock
Robert Hancock
Doug "TestZero" Hancox
Steven Hand
Jason Handy
Bryan Hanes
Matthew Hanley
Stephanie Hanmer
Christian Hansen
Joe Hanson
Matthew Harbour
Martin Harder
Leonard Hardiman
Will Harding
Michael Hardy
Phillip Hardy
Jason Hargrave

Jake Hargreaves
Nathaniel Harley
Ryan Harms
David Harries
Brad Harriger
Calum Harris
Emma-Lea Harris
Kyle Harris
Nicholas Harris
Sam Harris
Samantha Harris
Bradley Harrison
Michael Harrison
Tyler Harrison
Richard Harseno
Bob Hart
Jonny Hart
Adam Hartley
Marcus Hartwig
Ben Harvey
Caitlin Harvey
Lucy-Jane Harvey
Mike Harvey
Sam Harvey
Symi Harvey
Jamie Hasted
Aaron Hastings
Ådne Haugen
James Hauser
Lee Danger Hawken
Adam Hawkes
Chris Hawkins
Luke Hawkins
Ruffian Hawkins
John Haworth

Günter Haydinger
Anthony Hayes
Joe "Chef Sexcellence"
   Haynes
Thomas Haynes
Michael Hayward
Martin Hdbrg
Efan Headford
Tony Heald
Brian Christopher Healy
Connor Heard
Cameron Heide
Joseph Heimbecher
Rob Hein
Harry Hein-Hartmann
Daniel Heinrich
Heikki Heiska
Olli Heiskanen
Arnt Helge Helland
Mark Hellewell
Jake Helliwell
Patrick David Helm
Luke Helyer
Jacob Hemmerich
Ian Hemming
J Hemphill
Ryan Hemsley
Morton Hender
Thomas Henderson
Oliver Henkel
Benjamin Hennig
Fin Hennigan
Andrew Henry
Archie Henry
Paul Henry

Anthony Herana
Craig Heritage
Robert D. Hermann
Serena Householder
   Hernandez
Seb Heron
Tyrone Hesbrook
Alex Hesford
Elizabeth Hesketh
Robbie Hess
Joakim Dominic Hetland
Andy Hewitt
Joe Hewitt
James Heydecker
Henry Hibbs
Stan Hickinbottom
Alex Higgins
Marlon Montel Higgins
Richard Higgs
Anthony Highton
Luke Hill
Samuel Hill
Yannick Hill
Keiran Hillcoat
Dennis Hillmann
Ethan "Batman" Hilton
Michael Hilton
Stephan Hilzendegen
Daniel Hinchcliffe
Matthew Hine
Adam Hirst
Alex Hiscox
Jonathan Hoban
Adam Hobson
Samuel Hobson

Joshua Hodgkinson
Martin Hodgson
Matthew Hodkinson
Gunnar "Crazy_Borg" Hoffmann
Sean Hogan
Tom Hogan
Dean "Oh Bother" Hogarty
James Hogg
Harrison Hoggarth
Jacob Holdcroft
Scott Holder
Jordan "Thornbush42" Holloway
Mariel Holm
Dan Holmes
Ian Holmes
Michael Holmlund
Byron Holton
Steven Holtz
Calvin Holtzclaw
Sam Homand
Elizabeth Homer
Mark Honeyborne
Chris Honeyman
Shaun Hoolahan
Mark Hooton
Joey Hopkins
Austin Hoppes
Jordan Hoppes
Jeffrey Hordon
Taylor Horn
Rachele Horsfield
Zöe Horsham
Robert Horvath

Paul Hott
Luke Hough
Jacob Hougie
David Howard
Louise Howard
Ralph Howard
Drew Howell
Adam Howes
Paul Howes
Samuel Howitt
Yuyang Huang
Benjamin Hubbard
Caleb Hubble
Jett Hudjik
Connor Hudson
Shannon Hudson
Steven Hudson
Wayne Hudson
Daniel Huffman
Daniel Hughes
Dave Hughes
Jim Hughes
Kara Hughes
Kyle Hughes
Rebecca Hughes
Folko Hülsebusch
Joshua Humphrey
Chris Humphreys
Troy Hungerford
Arron Hunnisett
Bryan Hunt
Liam Hunt
Palex James Hunt
Walter John Hunt
Ben Hunter

Jeremy Huntink
Alex Hurding
Sean Hurley
Calvin Hurndell
Simon Hurst
Dale Hurton
Damian Hustyn
Francis Hutchinson
Rob Hutchinson
John Huxley
James Hynes
Jack James Iball
Daniel Ibbertson
Hristo Ignatov
Nicole Imber
Dylan Imeneo
Tobias "Rotzetool" Immel
Paul Immerzeel
John Imray
Eric Ingland
Karl Inglott
Carla M. Iovino
Alexander Iris
Jason Irving
Sara "Blufrog" Isakova
Goemon Ishikawa
Mohammed Issa
Jesper Ivarsson
Biliby Iwai
James Jackman
Luke Jackson
Luke Jackson
Tom Jackson
Oli Jacobs
Rowan Jacobs

Paul Jacobson
Justen Jagger
Ben Jakobek
Tuulia Jalava
Andy James
Bonnie James
Edward James
Greg James
Matt James
Hunter James
Marcus James
Thea Jamieson
Usman "Grey Butter" Jamil
Andrew Janosi
Lucia Janousek
Eddy Jansson
Felix Bonney Jarman
Michael Jarrett
Cheis Jarrett
Jimmy Jarshaw
Harry Jarvis
Russell Jarvis
Joshua Jasper
Tom Jasper
Jedrzej Jawor
Mike Jeavons
David Jelfs
Tony Jenkins
Rhys Jenkins
Wayne Jenkins
Jack Jenkinson
Parker Jensen
Dustin Jethro
Andrew Jewell
Espen Johannesen

Runa Johannsdottir
Kim Johansson
Brian Johnson
Charles Johnson
Chris "Chika" Johnson
Chris Johnson
Daryl Johnston
David "NFi" Johnson
Edward Johnson
Gram Johnson
Hayley Johnson
Kevin Johnson
Matthew Johnson
Oliver Johnson
Ryan Johnson
Louis Johnston
Nikki Johnston
Andreas Jokiel
Jon Jon
Ashley Jones
Cat Jones
Dean Jones
Gareth Jones
Jai Jones
Joachim Jones
Joel Jones
Jonathan Jones
Julie Iler Jones
Luke Jones
Martin Jones
Nicholas Jones
Oliver Jones
Phil Jones
Samuel M. Jones
Weeaboo Jones

Will Jones
Zachary David Jones
Victor Jonsson
Wes Jordan
Darren Joseph
Colin Josey
David Jozwiak
James Judd
Spencer Julian
Ged Jurga
Kah-Hoe K
Jürgen Kadlec (DC the
  cyBerfoxy)
Samuel "Sambomacho"
  Kadoche
James Kael
Sarah Kage
Geoffrey Kahler
Ossi Kajo
Alesja Kalinikova
Michele Kalva
Dennis Alexander Kanabey
ZH Kane
Arjun Shivanand Kannan
Kevin Karan
Artem Karapetyan
Jussi Karjalainen
Martin Karlsson
Alexander "Xan" Kashev
Alex Kassa
Kevin Katz
Philip Kaufmann
Adam Kavan
James/제임스 Kavanagh
Anders Kavla

James Kay
Stephen Kay
Matthew Keany
Kathleen Keating
Tom Keen
David Keenan
Kim Keeton
Scott Keith
Tobias Kelle
David Keller
Chris Kelley
Declan Kelly
Mark Kelly
Ryan Kelly
Joe Kemsley
Tayler Kemsley
Andrew Kennedy
Christina Kennedy
Ash Kenyon
Stefan Keranov
Nick Kerins
Fraser Kerr
(OfficialPirateFraser)
Jamie Kerr
Daniel Kerrigan
Amanda Kersshaw
Jae Kerwood
Patrick Ketaner
Ryan Ketteridge
Melissa Keursten
Kevin Kevane
Ian Kho
Khashayar Khoshrou
Wilf Kieran
Brandon Kiesling

Joanne Kilgour
Callum Kill
Peter Kimball-Evans
Andy Kimberley
Adrian Kind
Anton Kindestam
Daniel King
Ms. Gary Alexandria King
Iain King
Kevin King
Robert Kinns
Matthew Kirk
Ryan Kirkhoff
Jamie Kirkland
Luke Kirkpatrick
Chris Kirman
Parfyon Kirshnit
Simone Kirwan
Andre Kishimoto
Paul Kitching
Matt Kiteley
Fabian Klaetke
Adam Klassen
Michał Klaus
Benjamin Kleinfelter
Alex Kleinschmidt
Joe Klesczewski
Brian Kmak
Howard Knibbs
Paul Knibbs
Charlie Knight
James Knight
John Knight
Aaron Knight
Neil Knight

James Knill
Jared Knisely
Raphael Knott
Eldon Ko
Tony Koeffler
Stefan Koengeter
Thomas Kohl
Stefan "Chapi" Köhler
Tat Sing Kong
Dennis Konttaniemi
Janne Mikael Korhonen
Nikke Kostiainen
Manuel Kovats
Tim Kowalik
Sebastian Kozłowski
Jan Krause
Tjalfe Krause
Doug Krauss
Jens Krebs
Tobias Hernvig Kristensen
Zach Kromer
Matthew Kubicki
Zachary Kuhn
Mart Kuldkepp
Michael Kuligowski
Joseph Kuntz
Teemu Kurki
Jake Küssmaul
Sascha Kutzmann
Johan Kvande
Rachel L. Wedekind
Joshua Laber
Jessica Lach
Sam Ladner
Harmohn Laehri

Ville "jipostus" Lahtinen
Josh Lake
Chris Lakowicz
Lex Lamprey
Alexander Lane
Keith Lane
Alex Lang
George Langdon
Thomas Langford
Reece Langham
Markus Långström
Anne Lanham
Dominic Laoutaris-Brown
Nick LaPointe
Brian Largent
David Larkin
Alannah Larsen
Charlotte Larson
Emil Larsson
Elin Larsson
Pelle Larsson
Rowena Lashley
Jed Lath
Sam Lavin
Andrew Law
Keith Lawler
Jack Lawlor
David Lawrence
Lindsey Lawrence
Harry Lawrence
Saul Lawrence
Kris Lawton
Nicholas Lawton
Graham Layfield
Katie Leach

Kevin Leah
Alexander Leake
Darren Lean
Daniel Learmouth
Quentin LeBeau
Michel LeBlanc
Thomas LeBlanc
Jay Ledger
Alice Lee
Andy Lee
Corin Lee
Dennis Lee
Kris Lee
Matt Lee
Neil Lee
Richard Lee
Robert Leech
Rhys Leeke
Thomas Lees
James Lees
Zane Leff
Ryan LeGrand
Steven Leicester
Ian Leighly
Pentti Leino
Matthew Lennon
Brad Leonard
Janne Lepistö
Serena Leppanen
Alyssa Lerner
Stephan Lesch
Joseph Leslie
Dan Lesser
Jonathan Lester
Sam Leswisse

Alexander Lever
Adam Levitt
Bex Lewis
Bob Lewis
Christopher Lewis
Dan Lewis
Jacob Lewis
Kev Lewis
Matthew Lewis
Owen Lewis
Peter Lewis
Rhiannon Lewis
Ross Lewis
Sebastian Lewis
Carys Lewis-Watson
Francesco Lezi
Alex Lightfoot
Antti Juhani Liimatta
Stefan Lindfors
Ronald E. Lindhé
Fredrik Lindroth
Kristofer Lindsjö
Alexander Andrew Linton
George Lipyeat
Gunnar van Lit
Adam Little
Edward Little
Augustine Lloyd
Chi Lo
Kingston Lo
Brian Lobertini
Kristin Lockhart
Jamie Lockyer
Daz Lodge
Ryan & Bailie Loebs

Aaron Loessberg-Zahl
Arran Logan
Joseph Logan
Brandon Long
James Longley
Karl Johan Lõhmus
Dom Loraine
Maffiiee Lord
Moritz Lorey
Andrew Loughran
João Pedro H. G. Loureiro
Jon Lovegrove
James Loveridge
Ryan Low
Jenny Lowe
Jim Lowe
Stephen Lowe
Ruairi Lowery
Alexander Lowson
James Lowther
Anthony Lucas
Rob Lucas
Albert Lucia
Louis Luck
Nick Ludgate
Frank Ludlow
Stephen Ludlow
Andreas Lundgren
Steven Luo
Baustin Lux
Michael Lynch
Stephen Lynch
David Lyons
Korben Mabbs
Tamara Macadam

Sean MacBean
Angus Macdonald
Myles MacDonald
Nick Macey
George Machin
Hamish Mackay
Martin Macken
Ted Mackey
Curtis Mackie
Michael MacKinnon
Shawn MacRae
Katlin Maddox
John Madigan
Andrew Maeer
Robert Maehl
Patrick Magee
Venkat Mahadevan
Jehad Maher
Luke Robert James Main
Nathan Mainville
Robert Mair
Juho Majaniemi
Harrison Makepeace
Neil Malcolm
Nicholas Malthouse
Giorgio Malvone
Christopher "Chris" Man
Mike Manger
Zak Manley
Richard Manning
Hunter Manson
Per-Axel Mansson
Ian Marchant
Philip Marien
Thomas Mariucci

Joseph & Scarlett Markham
Iggy Markos
Richard Marr
Alan Marriott
Conor "Ronoc Mars" Marshall
Ethan Marshall
Helen Marshall
Philip Marshall
Rhys Marshall
Spencer Martell
Danny Martin
Graeme Martin
Kevin Martin
Law Martin
Robert Martin
Tim Martin
Tom A Martin
Stephen Martyn-Johns
Joe Marvin
Eric S Marynowski
Zak Mason
Kyle Massey
Michael Massey
Samantha Massey
Richee Mathwin
Lizzy Matterson
Colin Matthews
Lawrie Matthews
Daryl Mattinson
Whyle Mauriello
Christopher Mauro
Douglas Mawson
Matthew May
Paul May
Andreas Mayerhofer

Felix Mayfield
Maz Maz
Jacob Mc.
Paul McAteer
Chris McBride
Bernie McBurnface
Daniel McCabe
Stephen McCabe
Melissa Mccafferty
Kenneth Ellis McCall
James-Lachlan McCallum
Alice McCane
Matthew McCarroll
Paul McCarron
Jamie McCauley
Benjamin "Wile Man" McClune
Alasdair McCluskey
Kar McConnachie
Joey McConnell-Farber
Jonni McConville
William Mac McCorcle
Rachel McCormack
Matthew McCoy
Jack McCracken
Coire McCrystall
Kevin Paul McCullagh
Julie-Anne McCutcheon
Aaron McD
Robert McDaniel
Niall McDermott
Charlotte McDonald
Mark McDonald
Samantha McDonald
Thomas Mcdonald
Felix McDougle

John McElroy
Patrick McElwee
Liam McFarlane
Butterroac McFliggleblobb'n
Ross McGarvey
Conor McGhee
Raymond McGinty
Lee McGookin
Andrew McGregor
Niall McGuinness
Claire McHale
Elizabeth McIntivey
Andrew McIntyre
Logan McIntyre
Ian McIvor
Peter McKane
Sean Mckay
Erin Mckelvey
Darren McKenzie
Scott Mckerral
Theo McKinnon
John McLear
Bruce McLennan
Graham McLeod
Maranda McLeod and Mitch
    Crosby
Jennifer McLester
David McLintock
Hamish McMahon
Kevin McMullan
Craig Mcmurtry
Alex McNair
Henry McNamara
Amy McNeil
G. McNeil

Jamie McNeil
Alan McNeill
Cameron McPherson
Jason McPherson
Craig McSeveney
Nicholas McTaggart
Ryan McVicar
Daniel Mead
Eric Meadows
Jordan Meakin
Catherine Mearns
Dana Meddings
David Medina
Lukasz Medza
Chris Meeder
Jordan Meehan
Charles Meekins
Alexander Meijs
Tiffany Meldau
Ben Melluish
Dan Melluish
Andrew Melnick
Rev. Dr. Tomas Mendez
Uncle Mentuss
Nader Meradji
Ciaran Merrifield
Theodore Merrill
John Mestemacher
Ben Metcalf
Dan Michael
Kyriakos Michail
Abigail Michaud
Evan Michelsen
Connor Michie
Adam Campbell Milne

D. Mills
Danny Mills
Harris W. Miller
Ian Miller
Jack Miller
Kay Miller
Laura Mills
Luke Miller
Nathan Mlls
Scott Miller
Theo Minetos
Francisco Martínez Miranda
Nicholas Ryan Misturak
Bryan Mitchell
Callum Mitchell
Chris Mitchell
James Mitchell
Ross Mitchell
Hayley Mitrano
Christian Mittelstädt
Manuel Mizelli
Glenn Moase
Harrison Moenster
Daniel Moffatt
Kristoffer "Alctors" Mogensen
Hollie Moir
Neil Moir
Chloe Monaghan
David Monid
Simon Monk
Gonzalo Paolo Carrasco
    Montanares
Paul "Monty" Montgomery
Robert Montgomery
Taylor Montoya

Gabriel Moody
Jordan Mooney
Andrew Moore
Arthur Moore
Daniel Moore
Dimitri Moore
Richard Moore
William Moore
Jonathon Moran
Rachel Moran
Johan Moremalm
Carl Morgan
Jamie Morgan
Tim Morgan
Dominic Morley
Chris Morris
Dan Morris
Elijah Morris
Grace Morris
Richie Morris
Drew Morrison
Grant Morrison
Harry Morrow
Aaron Morton
The Mother
Andreas Mottl
Sarah Mouhajer
Will Mower (ProfSquirrel_)
MrBrick MrBrick
Laura Muehlbauer
Wayne Muff
Darren "Weebl" Muir
Mike Müllejans
Maike Muller
James Mulvale

Jason Mumford
Joseph Mumford
Rose Mundie
Charlie Munns
Shanneen Murphy
Miranda Murphy
Patrick Fisher Murphy
Sarah Murphy
Daniel Murray
Ewen Murray
Andy Murrell
Joseph Murse
Shalott Muse
Kacper Musialkowski
John Mylan
Sindri Myr
Michaela Nachtigall
Benoit Nadeau
Phillip Naeser
Adam Nail
Billy Naing
Andrew Nairn
John Nash
Mark Nation
Michael Neal
Stuart Neal
Alexander Ruben Neave
Chuck Neely
Ivo Nelissen
Dylan Nelson
Michael Nelson
Shaun Nelson
Darrow Nemecek-Gulack
Absurd Nerd
Trevor Neubeck

Aaron Neville
Matty "Cirno" Newell
Elliot Newman
Kate Newman ⓨ
Stu Newnham
Rob Newstead
Alexander Newton
Tony Nguyen
Natalie Nicholas
Dan Nicholls
Robert Nicholson
Ed Nickel
Chris Nicklin
Alexander Nicolas
Martin Walberg Nicolaysen
Gerard Nieborg
Derek Nielsen
J Nielsen
Simon "FischOderAal"
    Nienhaus
Alice Nietgen
Marie-Jose Nieuwkoop
Va Nilla
Joel Nilsson
Mark "Fawlkes" Nisbet
Michael Nisbet
Sam Nissen
Finlay Niven
Dan Nixon
Cain Noble-Davies
Nathaniel Noda
David Noddle
Antonia Noel-Buxton
Mitch Noon
Rebecca Noonan

Matti Nordström
Colin Norris
Joshua Norris
Bryana Norstedt
Matt North
Steve Northcott
James Norton
Kirk Norton
Andrew Nosler
Jens Nøstvik
Carsten Nottebohm
David "Twisted" Nottingham
Patrick Novak
Elizabeth Nuhfer
Adie Nunn
Andy Oakley
Loz Oakley
Joanna Oakley
Anthony Robert O'Brien
Mike Obrien
Peter O' Brien
Eileen O'Byrne-Hudson
Oliver Ockenden
Dan O'Connor
Darkūūmbāus Ocoorime
Ivan Odintsoff
Marc Ó'Dubhlinn
Britt Oertel
Liam O'Flynn
David O'Grady
Jack O'Keeffe
Iver Oknes
Rose Oldershaw
Ronan O Leary
Joshua Oliva

Adam Olivari
Oliver Oliver
Brian K. Olsen
Ben Olson
Cameron T. Olson
Erik Olson
Par Olsson
DJ Omnifusion
Mark O'Neill
Garry O'Neill
Cormac O'Neill
Ted O'Quilley
Michael Ordidge
Alex Orman
Jeff Orr
Ryan Mark Orrell
James Osey
Paul Osman
Maciej Ostaszewski
Daniel Österby
Andreas Filskov Kirk
    Østergaard
Carsten Otte
Paige Overbury
Danny Owen
Scott Owens
Sam Owens
Alastair Meengamer Oxby
Andrew Oxford
Sean Oxspring
Hakan Özalp
Frank P.
Kirstie "Kujatus" Parr
Sergio P Pereira
Hazel Page

Steven Page
Matt Pagliaro
Markus Pahl
Stelle Luna Star Paige
Daniel Palfrey
Daniel Palm
Alan Palmer
Ty Palmer
Gunnar Pálsson
Arjen Pander
Nep Pangilinan
Kostas Papadakis
Stelios Papanastasiou
Austin Paquette
Lucas Pardue
Ryan Parish
Allan Parker
Jamie Parker
Josh Parker
Robert Parker
Cassie Parkes
Graham Parks
Jacob Parley
David Parr
Jon Parry
Karl Parry
anthony parsons
Martin Partridge
Jacqueline Pasco
Anthony Pascone
Brian S Paskin
Patrick Pastolero
Kiran Patel
Mark Patelunas
Mark Paterson

Terence Paterson
James Paton
Patrick Patrick
William Paxton
Kyle J Peace
Andrew Peak
Emily Peak
Jay Pear
Ayase-Lewis Pearce
Gareth Pearce
Nick Pearce
Iain Pearson
William George Peckham
Katharina Alberta Pedersen
Erica Pegg
Ruben Pender
John Penney
Laurent Pépin-Julien
Jacob Peplinski
Elena Pereira
Richard Perrins
Sam "Graphikal" Persaud
Peskeh Peskeh
Carl Peters
Dan Peters
Thomas Petersen
Eric Peterson
Joshua Peterson
Simon Peterson
Joe Petner
Jon Petrusev
Sebastian Pettersson
Sten Jørgen Pettersen
Matt Petts
Devin Philipps

Frederick Phillips
Jamie A S Phillips
Jon Phillips
Thomas Phillips
Connor Philpott
Severin Pick
Elliott Pickett
Dixie Pickles
Jon Pidduck
Fingal Pierce
Ross Pigrum
Mateusz Pikora
Adam Pilborough
James Pilcher
Holly Pilgrim
Ben Pinkerton
Simon Pinkerton
Gemma Pinney
Laura Pinnick
Harry Pipes
David John Pires
Jacob Pitcock
Valentino Pizzi
Michael Plasket
Jeremy Platt
Haydn Plumb
Chris Plumridge
Mark Pocock
Mathew Poehlman
Callum Pogson
Michael Polcari
Daniel Polcari
Gabriel Pollard
Alastair Pollitt
Dean Poole

Ivan Popov
Amir Porat
Ian Port
Chris Porter
Lewis Porter
Matthew Porter
Steven Porter
Thomas Porter
Tim Porter
Juan Postel
Aidan Potter
Daniel Potter
Jon Potter
William Potts
Ewen Pountney
Alan Pow
Matt Powell
Aaron Powers
Adrian Powici
Mats Powlowski
Samantha Poynter
Jurate Pozeraite
John Pratt
Kieran Pratt
Matt Preiss
Ethan Prendergast
Michael Pressburg
Bobby Lee Price
Callum Price
Cameron Price
Ian Price
Lee Price
Thomas Price
Sam Pridige
Alex Pringle

Dan Proença
Steffen Seth Prohn
Mitchell Proud
Max Pruce
Patrick Prudlik
Kevin Pryke
Michael Cody Przeslica
Edward Puckering
Brent Puet
Matthew Pull
Jillian Pullara
Dan Punter
Justin Puopolo
Jas Purewal
Tim Purt
Tyler Puryear
Aaron Puzey
Huan Quayle
Zachary Quick
Jamie Quinlan
Jeremy Quinn
Daniel Quinones
Kevin Rademacher
Olivia Radford
Andrew Radlett
Angus Rae
Nicholas Ragan
Mikko Rajanen
Matan Ram
Eric G. Ramirez
Sarah Ramsay
Bobby Rank
Nath Raspin
David Ratcliffe
Rae Raven

Luke Raymond
William "Elliot" Rayner
Christina Razzi
Gordon Ream
Blainy RedCat
Ashley Reed
Owen Reed
Gaz Rees
Jamie Rees
Joshua Reeson
Samuel Reeve
Jay Reichman
Craig Reid
Shannon Reid
Craig Reilly
Liam Reilly
David Reinhardt
Thibaut Renaux
james Reuben
Gabe Reyna
John Reynolds
Matthew Reynolds
Josh Rice
The Rt Hon Mr James
    Marshall Harrison Rich Esq.
Troy Gordon Rich
Craig Richards
Dan Richards
Stephen Richards
    (RetroUnlim.com)
Ashley Richardson
Justin Richardson
Nick Richardson
Jonah Richcardson
Alex Richmond

Jake Emile Richmond
James E Richmond
Lisa Richmond
Liam Riddell
Sam Riddell
Chris Rider
Jonathan Rigby
Daniel Riley
Aidan Riley
Nicholas Ring
Christopher Ringe
Zachary Rippe
Jess M. Rivera
Jon-Carlos Rivera
Christopher Rivett
Martin Rix
Ian Robb
Cynthia Roberson
Andy Roberts
Benjamin Roberts
Harry Roberts
Iain "Chumpyman" Roberts
Kelly Roberts
Louis D Roberts
Rhys Roberts
Russell Roberts
Stacy Roberts
Stuart Roberts
Gary Roberts (Related)
Steven Roberts (Related)
James Robertson
Corey Robillard
Aaron Robinson
Alexander James Robinson
Jack Robinson

Jacob Robinson, Happy
    Birthday!
Jason Robinson
Paul Robinson
Scott Robinson
Zachary Robinson
Lara Robinson-Hoyer
John Roblin
Thomas Robson
Paddy Roche
Paul Roche
Jackson Roché
Gregory Rockcliffe-Smith
Iain Rockliffe
Lee Rodger
Shaun Rodger
Harry Rodgers
Andrew Rodland
Stian Rødland
Marek Rogalski
Adam Rogers
Kole Rogers (The Dark and
    Mysterious)
The Rohe Brothers
Andrew Rohl
Victor Portela Romero
George Ronksley
David Rose
Joshua Rosebrough
Lea Roselli
Scott Rosevear
Andrew Scoundrel Ross
Jack Ross
Cory Roth
David Rourke

Chris Rowland
Mark Rowley
Stephen Rowley
James "Llama Likes Gaming"
    Rowsell @CoolJWR100
Joey Rucker
Will Rucker
Brad Rudacille
Maxi Rüdiger
Jonny Ruff
Lukas Russell
Johan Rutberg
Toni Ru□a
Alex Ryan
Kian Ronan Ashton Ryan
Megan Ryan
Sam Ryan
Sean Ryan
Justin Rybinskì
Iikka Ryynänen
TJ Saari
Sam Sackett
Phil Sadler
John Sadowski
Johan Saf
Matthew Sager
Aaron Saine
Salvador R. Salcido
Ramon Saldivar
Sarah Sale
Jeremy Salisbury
Keenan Salla
Rikki Salmon
Calum Salmond
Colin Salvona

Ivan Sanchez
Tammy Sandeen
Hugh Sandeman
James Danger Sanders
Scott Sanderson
Isak Roald Sandvik
Michael Santos
Mark Sargent
Alex Sarll
Callum Sarracino
Rosaria Sasso
Martin Saul
Alexander Saunders
Alix Saunders, the
    Magnificent & Spectacular
    (Asauz)
Neil Sawell
Adam Sawyers
Tomás Scaiola
Dave Scammell
Matthew Schacht
William Scharmach
Oliver Schawohl
John Scheinler
Kevin Schepler
Lucas Scheuenstuhl
Michael Schiciano
Michael Schlechta
xeetsh (Max Schmitt)
Eliza Schnabel
Austin Scholl
Andrew Schonenberger
Andreas Schouten
Alex Schramke
Michael Schultz

Daniel Schulz
Tristan Schulze
Jonathan Schuman
Alex Scott
Austin Scott
Hamish Scott
Jenny Scott
Kayleigh Scott
Mitchell Scott
Philip Scott
Robert Scott
Tim Scott
Katie Scrivener
Paul Scullion
seagull (www.seagull.io)
Owen Searfoss
Jack Seaton
Paul Sebert
Jonas Segura
Claudiu Selar
Liam Self
Terho Selin
Mica Sellers
Dell Selter
Ben Jammin Semple
Chaz Serir
Dylan Servilla
Steven Serzant
Matthias Seul
Oliver Shackleton
Mehdi shahmehdi327
Roger Shanks
Ethan Sharon
Christopher Sharp
Paul Sharp

James Shaw
John Shawler of Amigos
    Podcast
¯°·._.· Tⅰᴍόᴛһ¥ ρɑᴛʀⅰ¢Ḱ
    ѕḣᴣᴣḣ¥ ·._.·°¯
Sean Shelley
Matt Shepherd
Gary Sheppard aka Dominoid
Kelvin Sherman
Grant Shipcott
Shared Shirts
Stephen Shiu
Pasha Shmuylovich
Jaime Shuminski
Jon Shute
James Shuter
Kaspar Shyjka
Emily Siddle
Jonathan Siddle
Dave & Holly Siederer
Matt Sieker
Matthew Sigmond
Maiju Siltaniemi
Jorge "punkmaniac" Silva
Duste Silverfin
Dan Silvester
Kieron Sim
Mark Simister
Paul Simkowski
Andrew Simmonds
David Simmonite
Henrik Simonsen
Verity Simpson
Daniel Simpson
Joe Simpson

Lauren Simpson
Louise Simpson
Michael Simpson
Ryan Simpson
Adam Sims
Cord Sims
Iain Sinclair
Alexander Singler
Daniel Singleton
Antti Sirviö
Charles Skeavington
Steven Skelly
Søren Skov
Richard Skrei
Misty Skylight
Dave Slater
Mollie Slater
Stephen Slatky
Ben Slee
Joshua Sloane
Eva Slusher
James Slusher, Jr.
Alexander Smakman
Jimmy Smallman
Alexander Smith
Andrew Smith
Anthony J Smith
Benjamin James Smith
Christopher Smith
Colin Smith
Daniel Smith
Dean Smith
Emma Smith
Hazel Smith
Jessica Smith

Joel Smith
Josh Smith
Joshua Smith
Isaac Smith
Ryan Smith
Scott Smith
Simon Smith
Stuart Smith
Robert Smith
Sam Smith
Steve Smith
Zaq Smith
Leon Smulders
Michael Smythe
Charley Snape
Natalie May Snook
Susan Snow and Justin
    Waskiewicz
Ryan Snyder
Markel Soikes
Stian Solli
Alexandra Solomon
David Somers
Aleanne Sommer
Ian Soon
Stuart Sopko
Mario Sorgente
Matthew "ReplayRetro" Sorrell
Natasha Soutar
Chloe Spencer
Izaak Spencer
James Spencer
Samuel Spencer
Sean Spencer
Rick Spermon

Ellis Spice
Joel Spicer
Liam Spinage
Jamie Spong
Aaron Sporer
Mark Sprusen
Marcus Spry
John Squyers
Alasdair J. Stainer
Ashley Stancill
Gabrielle Stanley-Sims
Dan Stanton
Rusty Stark
Andrew Steele
Sam Steele
Casper Steen
Matvei Stefarov
Emily Stell
David Stelling
Jens-Ejnar Stephansen
Nick Stephens
Robert E. Stephenson
Callum Steven
Alec Stevens
Hannah Stevens
Jason Stevens
Lee Stevens
Andrew Stevenson
Robert Spencer Stewart
U.E. Callum T. Stewart
Isaac Stidham
Kieran Still
Matthew Stobbs
Sam Stockdale
Kevin Stock-Kitzerow

Matthew Stogdon
Michael Stokes
Sondre Stølen
Curits Stollery
James Stone
Connor Storr
Dan Stott
Joshua Stough
Katie Stowell
Samuel Stracey
Robert Straub
Michael Strawson
Kevin Street
Matthew Streuli
Ulf Strömberg
Daniel Stuart
Will Stubbs
Wong Su Jun
Matthew Suconick
Antti-Jussi Suksi
Kent Sullivan
Alex Summers
Lee Summers
Paul Summers
Sean Suprenant
Tim Suter
Graham Sutherland
Scott Sutherland
Matt "Echo" Sutton
James Sutton
John Sutton
Wilhelm Svenselius
Lucy Swan
Liam Swann
C.J. Sweatt

Lewis Sweeney
Kevin Swidzinski
Lyndon Swift
Stephen Swift
Jennifer Swindells
Stephen Swires
David Symmons
Leah Elizabeth Szpak
Marc T
Ryan Tabbner (Turnip)
Nulani t'Acraya
Gábor Waitforit Takács
Timo Takalo
Luke Takoto Burns-Luckhurst
Aidan Talbot
Ben Talbot
Zak Talbot
Toni Tammisalo
Ian Tanswell
Ashley Tasker (Ashlo122)
Tuomas Taskila
Ezra Tassone
Allen Tate
Kayleigh Tate
Jose Taveras
Chris Taylor
Christopher "Ceryndrion"
    Taylor
David Taylor
Duncan Taylor
Grant Taylor
Hannah Taylor
James Taylor
Joel Taylor
Kat Taylor

Lee Taylor
Matt Mallory Taylor
Maxwell Taylor
Peter J. L. Taylor
Ross Taylor
Stuart Taylor
Glyn Tebbutt
Harry Tedeschi
Finn Tempo
John Testa
Matt Tester
Leonie Texier
Morgan The Bloodedge
Daniela Thelen
Sian Thirkettle
Theresa Thirkill
William Thode
Daniel "Soup" Thomas
Emily Thomas
Garan Thomas
James Thomas
Randy Thomet
Benjamin George James
    Leaver Thompson
Daniel Thompson
Derek Thomson
Jack Thompson
James Thompson
Isaac Thompson
Katherine-Louvain Thompson
Katie Thompson
Lewis Thompson
Naomi Thompson
Tyler Thompson
Robert Thomson

Alex Thorn
Benjamin Thornton
Brandon Thornton
Raphael Thoulouze
Ben Thrussell
Kyle Thurman
Chris Thursfield
Matthew Thwaites
Daniel Tighe
Sophie Tillbrook
Owen Tilling
Jamy Timmermans
Hans Timmers
Alex Tindall
Ben "the bespectacled"
    Tindall
Michael Tindall
Ted Tinker
matthias tirednsore
Douglas Titchmarsh
Joann Tober
Matt Tobin
Jake Todd
Tom Todd
Andrew Todhunter
Ville Toivanen
Nathan Tokala
Charles Toler
William Tomkinson
Paul Tomlin
Calvin Tomlinson
Charlie Tomlinson
Will Tommo
Johann-Mattias Toom
Dan Tootill

Rob Toplis
Mark Topp
Niko Torkkel
Espen Torseth
Ryan Townsend
Adam Towsey
Dave Toyne
Matt Trafford
Miika Tranberg
Richard Tranter
Ross Tregaskis
Lowell Treude
Leonardo Trevas
Hollie Tribbeck
Daniel Tribe
Joe Trigg
John T. Trigonis
Stuart Trotter
William Truong
Jon Truran
Hector Ttofa
Matt Tucker
James Tudhope (Tuddy)
Will Tudor
Zoltan Tudos
Peter Malcolm Tullett
Faye Tunnicliff
Andrew Turcich
James Turner
Josh Turner
Matt Turner
Sean Turner
Shareef Turner
Alex Turnpenny
Jess Turpin

Richard Twyman
Jeffrey McClain Tyson
Joseph Ullmann
Kay Are Ulvestad
Josh Underdown
Percy Underwood
Lloyd Unruh
Ryan Unruh
Connor Unsworth
Darek V.-J.
Aiden Vaines
Mika Väinölä
Marcello Valastro
Ernesto Francisco Arias
    Valverde
Carlos Gutiérrez Valerio
Estevan Valle
Michael Vallender
Martijn van Antwerpen
Werner Van Campenhout
Remco van den Heuvel
Jeroen van der Velden
Yves Van Hoof
Misja van Laatum
Davy Van Obbergen
Isaac Van Ristell
Wouter Vander Waeren
Alan Vanhoven
Luke Varley
Ruben Varne
Daven Vasishtan
Alex Vaughan
James Stuart Vaughan
Christopher Veach
Leo Veloz

Mark Vent
Colin Venters
Tatiana Ventura
Timothy Verheyn Jr.
BjøRn Vermöhlen
Robin Verschoren
Paco Verschut
Dylan Veysey
Harry Vigers
Markus Vikmanis
Mark Vincent
Jernej Virag
Frankie Viturello
Jose Vizcaino
Daniel von Oesen
Emily VonSydow
Yury Voronin
George Vosper
Jamie Voss
vpolp vpolp
Crystal Vu
Steven Vuong
Benjamin Waas
Alexander Waddell
Adam Wade
Evan Wagoner
Neal Wahlfield
Bradley Wainwright
Emilia Wake
Daniel Wakefield
Barry Wakenshaw
Thomas Waldo
Josh Walker
Paul Walker
Thomas Walker

Trevor Walker
Ryan Walker (nine3hundred)
Matthew "J Wall" Wallace
Michael Elton Wallace
Sam Wallace
Robb Wallace
Thomas Wallace
Jono Wallcraft
Julien Wallet-Houget
Mark Wallis
Matthew Wallis
Mathew Walls
Simon Xavier Walmsley
Jorge Walsh
Kieran Walsh
Jared Walske
Eric Walstrom
David Walter
Mark Walton
Benjamin Walton
Daren Walz
Thomas Wampler
Marcus Wan
Mark Wane
Peter Waples
Hannah Ward
John Ward
Lawrence Ward
Steven Ward
Ellie Ware
Marc Warner
Stu Warner
Timmo Warner
David Warren
Ben Warrender

David Warrington
Joshua Washburn
Cody S. Watkins
Dominic Watling
Marc Watson
Neil "poonab" Watson
Ryan Watson
Thomas Watson
Stewart Watters
Bethany Webb
Christopher Webb
Dylan Webb
Richard Webb
Björn Weber
Ben Webster
Russell Elliott Webster
Thomas Webster
Oscar Weckström
Oliver Wedgwood
Michael Weeks
Max Wegner
Bryan Weights
Ewan Weir
Stewart Weir
Russell Welfare
Joey Weller
Todd Weller
Kristofer Wells
Kyle Wells
Reese Wells
Robert Wells
Robert "Weaselspoon" Wells
Tom Wells
Rhys Welsby
Sean Welsh

Stephen Welsh
David Wendt Jr.
Jens Wengman
Tanner Wenzel
Roland Wenzel
Adam Wesley
Willem Wesseldijk
Callum West
Ryan West
Andrew Westgate
Chris Weston
Samantha Westwood
Elizabeth Wetton
Joseph Wharmby
Andy Whatman
Callum Wheatley
Mark Wheeler
Nicholas Wheeler
Phoebe Wheeler
Flynn Whelan
Paul Whelan
Steve Whipp
Nathan Whipps
Russell Whiskin
Katie Whitby
Marc Whitcombe
Alicia White
Grant White
Jason White
Skylar White
Stephen White
Richard Whitechest
Anthony Whiteley
Douglas Whiteside
Dani Whitford

Ben Whiting
Sam Whiting
David Whitney
David Whitten
Pete Whitton
Luke Wholey
David Whyld
Tom Whyte
Matthew Wieker
Keith Wiggins
Hannah Wigmore
Wout "Tenshi" Wijker
Pekka Wikman
Travis Wikoff
Gavin Wilcock
Nicola Wilcox
Rhys Wilcox
Jake Wiles
Timothy Wiles
Dominic Wiley
Stephen Wilkicki II
Ben Wilkinson
Kai Arne Willerud
Andrew Williams
Brenden Williams
Calvin Williams
Caylen Williams
Dafydd Williams
Damien Williams
Dave Williams
Giles Williams
Glyn Williams
Harry Williams
Holly Williams
Jamie Williams

Matthew Williams
Michael Williams
Mike Williams
Olivia Williams
Simon Williams
Tom Williams
Tristan Williams
Jake Williamson
Katie Williamson
Sean Williamson
Steve Williamson
Adam Willighan
Nikolas Willingham
Andrew Wilson
Bob Wilson
Frank Wilson
Lorna Wilson
Martin Wilson
Mat Wilson
Nicholas Wilson
Robert Wilson
Ruairidh Wilson
Steven Wilson
Joe Wilson-Palmer
Peter Wiltshire
Jessica Winch
Josh Windus
Michael Winn
Chris Winter
Adam Witney
Billy Witton
Joel Woelke
Auld Wolf
James Wolfe
Sasha Wolf-Powers

Gregory Wolking
Wojciech Wołoszczak
Martin Wolters
Joel Womack
Pete Wonnacott
Andrew Wood
Ben Wood
Edward Wood
Sarah Wood
Yvette Wood
David Woodley
Andrew Woodrup
Joanna Woodworth
Nathan Wookey
Katie Woolford
peter woolford
Christian-Philipp Worring
John Worster
Thomas Worster
Eddy Worthington
Thomas Wren
Alexander Wright
Dakota Wright
David William Wright
Glen Wright
Jeffrey Wright
Matthew Wright
Samuel Wright
Mikko Wrightson
Peter Wroot
Kenny Wu
Zak Wyeth
Jonathan Wynter
Tré X
Krista Yabe

David Yarnold
Ben Yates
Peter Yates
William Yates
Oladapo Yeku
Timo Yli-Rosti
Joanne York
Anthony Young
David Young
Jonny Young
Scott Young
Tim Young
Zac Youngdale
Amy "AutumnSounds" Yue
David Yuill-Kirkwood
Alec Z
Efrain Zamora
zard1 zard1
Christoph Zeitz
Jackson Zellmer
Alex Zevenbergen
Rui "John Money" Zhi
Greg Ziegler
Jakub Ziemkiewicz
Nick Zignauskas
Jeremy Zitnik
Walter Zollinger
Elric Zufan
Bart Zuidgeest. Someone
    You've Probably Never
    Heard Of. Also someone
    whose last name you'll find
    unpronounceable if you're
    not Dutch. You know, this
    text box seems to go on

forever. I wonder how
long I can make my name.
Maybe get the entire book
in here...
ЗлuΖ ソウザ